The Yles of O...

A Scale of Miles

Caithnes

Stratho Leith

SUTERLAND

marble mountains of Sutherland

Strath Carron

Rosse

Tarbartnes
Tarbart

Stranauern

Cathes

Nes head

Dunesbe head

Rossmark

Elgin
Ainzia

Boena

Buquhan

Aberdone
New Aberdone

MURAY

Strathbogy

Gare

Kildrumy

Badgenoth

L. Marria
L. Muik

Mernia
Glembaray

Athole

Brethin

Red head

Dunkell

Perth
Strath Erne

THE GERMANE

Fife nes

SEA

Lac. Lomond

Menteith

Dunblain

Firth alban rium

The Bale

Sterling

Striueling

Lenox

Glasguo

Edinburgh

The Mar

Barwick

LOUTHIANE

Twedale

Kyle

Douglas dale

Anand ale

Nythes dale

Tiuedale

ches

PART OF

ENGLAND

Anna Queene of Great Brittii, Fraunce and Ireland.

Charles Duke of York and Albany.

Performed by Iohn Speed and are to be sold in Popes head alley by Iohn...

MONTROSE

James Graham, 1st Marquess of Montrose, attributed to William Dobson (National Galleries of Scotland)

MONTROSE

C.V. Wedgwood

ST. MARTIN'S PRESS · NEW YORK

First published in the United Kingdom in 1952

First published in the United States of America in 1995

ISBN 0-312-12584-4

Library of Congress Cataloging-in-Publication Data applied for

Endpapers: detail from The Kingdome of Scotland *by John Speed, 1610*

Printed in Great Britain by
Butler and Tanner, Frome, Somerset.

To
John Julian Wedgwood

CONTENTS

List of Illustrations   *viii*

Foreword   *xi*

Chapter 1:   Silver Arrows and Golden Opinions   *1*

Chapter 2:   For God, Covenant and Country   *14*

Chapter 3:   King Charles or King Campbell?   *31*

Chapter 4:   Hope Deferred   *45*

Chapter 5:   The Chase Begins   *61*

Chapter 6:   A Far Cry to Loch Awe   *76*

Chapter 7:   Heroic Ventures   *86*

Chapter 8:   Triumph   *99*

Chapter 9:   Disaster   *110*

Chapter 10:   Exile and Return   *126*

Chapter 11:   The Last Victory   *143*

Epilogue: The Great Marquess   *156*

A Note on Books and Sources   *161*

Index   *163*

ILLUSTRATIONS

Montrose, attributed to William Dobson	Frontispiece
1. The young Montrose by George Jamesone	xii
2. Montrose's archery medal	1
3. A copy of James Gordon's map of St Andrews	2
4. The Old College of Glasgow	3
5. Montrose's entry in the Glasgow College archives	3
6. Montrose's sword	5
7. Kinnaird Castle	7
8. Tom Sydserf by Michael Wright	8
9. Charles I by Sir Robert Strange	11
10. James, Marquess of Hamilton	12
11. Title page of the Scottish Book of Common Prayer	15
12. St Giles' Church	16
13. John Leslie by George Jamesone	18
14. Alexander Henderson, attributed to Van Dyck	23
15. General Alexander Leslie, attributed to George Jamesone	25
16. George Gordon and his wife	26
17. Huntly Castle	27
18. The Old Bridge of Dee	29
19. Engraving of the Pacification of Berwick	30
20. Berwick town plan by John Speed	32
21. Archibald Campbell by David Scougall	34
22. Montrose's letter to Charles I, 26 December 1639	37
23. Sir Archibald Napier by George Jamesone	38
24. Lady Napier, attributed to Adam de Colone	38
25. Newcastle town plan by John Speed	39
26. Edinburgh Castle	42

27. The raising of the Royal Standard   46

28. Henrietta Maria, after Van Dyck   48

29. York town plan by John Speed   49

30. Christ Church, Oxford   51

31. The Solemn League and Covenant   55

32. Carlisle town plan by John Speed   58

33. Prince Rupert by Gerard Honthorst   59

34. Glen Tilt near Blair Atholl end   62

35. Plan of the Campaign of Tippermuir and Perth   65

36. Plan of the Battle of Aberdeen   66

37. Montrose's letter to Aberdeen Town Council   68

38. Aberdeen's reply to Montrose   69

39. Lord Marischal's letter to the Earl of Argyll   71

40. Re-enactment of the Battle of Fyvie   73

41. Loch Awe   77

42. Plan of the Campaign of Inverlochy   78

43. Glencoe in winter   79

44. Inverlochy Castle   83

45. George Gordon   88

46. Plan of the Campaign of Dundee and Auldearn   90

47. Plan of the Battle of Auldearn   93

48. Plan of the Campaign of Alford   95

49. The Bridge of Alford   96

50. Plan of the Battle of Alford   97

51. Plan of the Campaign of Kilsyth   99

52. Plan of the Battle of Kilsyth   102

53. Charles I's proclamation, 18 August 1645   104

54. Bothwell Castle   106

55. Montrose's letter to Lord Ogilvie, 28 August 1645   107

56. General David Leslie   110

57. Plan of the Campaign of Philiphaugh   112

58. Bond by provost and baillies of Jedburgh to John Stewart 113

59. Newark Castle   114

60. Deposition by the provost, bailles and council of Glasgow
before the Earl of Lanark, 29 September 1645   116–17

61. Site of Kincardine Castle   119

62. Montrose's letter to Charles I, 2 June 1646   120–1

63. Magdalen, Lady Montrose   124

64. Title page of George Wishart's book on Montrose   128

65. Execution of Charles I   129

66. Charles II at The Hague by Cornelius Janssen   131

67. Elizabeth Stuart, Queen of Bohemia   133

68. Montrose, attributed to Gerard Honthorst   134

69. Cartoon of Charles II and the Scots   137

70. Plan of the Campaign of Carbisdale   139

71. Ardvreck Castle   141

72. Skibo Castle   144

73. Montrose paraded through Edinburgh, by James Drummond   148

74. Archibald Johnston by George Jamesone   151

75. Lady Elizabeth Erskine   152

76. Montrose's execution   154

77. Montrose's statue in St Giles' Church   159

78. Montrose's insignia   160

Picture numbers 35, 36, 42, 46, 47, 48, 50, 51, 53, 57 and 70 are taken from John Buchan, *Montrose* (Thomas Nelson and Sons Ltd, 1931)

FOREWORD

I enjoyed writing this book, partly because, following Montrose's extraordinary campaigns took me on foot into some of the most beautiful parts of Scotland, but chiefly because I enjoyed studying Montrose himself.

An accomplished youth, a brilliant amateur soldier and inspired guerilla leader, a not inconsiderable poet, a man of great courage, integrity and nobility of mind, he met a horrible death with exemplary fortitude and stands out in the annals and legends of the Civil Wars of Scotland as a pattern of the epic hero.

I am happy that the publication of this fully illustrated edition brings forward once more the exciting and moving story of his life and death enriched by visual material from a wide variety of sources.

C.V. Wedgwood

The young Montrose by George Jamesone (In the collection of the Earl of Southesk)

CHAPTER ONE

SILVER ARROWS AND GOLDEN OPINIONS

J ames Graham, Earl of Montrose, was not quite seventeen when in July 1629 he won the silver arrow at St Andrews University for the second time. The silver arrow was the coveted prize for the best archer, and every student with skill enough to manage a bow competed for the honour. It was a popular victory, for Montrose was generous. The first time he had won the arrow he had entertained the archers to cakes and wine with a concert of drums and pipes. On this occasion he had invited them to a breakfast of roast mutton before the contest. When it was over and he was proclaimed the winner for a second time, he gave another feast. The boys who carried the quivers and the men who marked the targets were not forgotten.

Ever since he had come to St Andrews, and even earlier, Montrose had done things in style. His friends teased him because he trained his racehorse on a diet which included white bread and beer. The beggars in the streets and the caddies on the golf links knew him for an open-handed gentleman. The servants who brought him presents from his numerous relations – a fresh trout; a haunch of venison or a brace of partridges – never went away

The silver medal archery prize won by Montrose while at St Andrew's University (Department of Manuscripts, St Andrew's University)

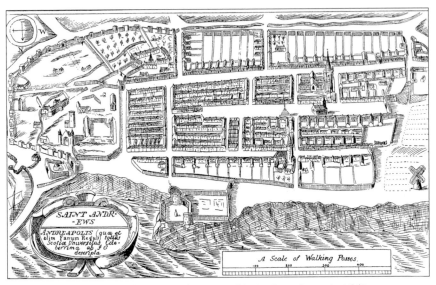

A later copy of James Gordon's map of St Andrews drawn in 1642

unrewarded. The gardeners in the neighbourhood of St Andrews knew that they could count on a piece of silver in thanks if they brought some rare or beautiful flower to show to him. Young as he was, he was already a patron of literature and learning. He had generously helped William Lithgow, the Scottish traveller and poet, and he had given a large sum of money for books to the High School at Glasgow where he had received his earlier education.

Montrose rode gracefully, was skilful with his rapier and played a good game of golf. He was also sensitive to beauty, to colours, words and landscape. His rooms at St Andrews were hung with curtains of red figured damask; there were velvet cushions on the chairs and embroidered cloths on the tables. There was also a cabinet of books, handsomely bound and carefully arranged. He had collected what pleased him best. For his studies there were the usual grammars and classics, the usual philosophical, moral or historical treatises; Caesar's commentaries, of course; Lucan's poems, and the *Life of Alexander the Great* by Quintus Curtius. But there were also works on chivalry, tales

2

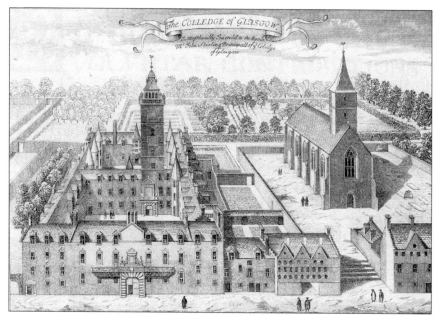

The Old College of Glasgow at the end of the seventeenth century.

*Montrose's entry in the Glasgow College archives: 'To be givin be me James Erle of Montrose for
the help of the Building and Librarie of the Colledge of Glasgow the sowm of Four Hundreth
merks. Subscryved with my hand at Edinburgh 19 October 1632.*
Montrois
{Payed 16 November 1634, and debursed be the Principall.}'

of adventure and romance, Tasso's great heroic poem, *Jerusalem Delivered*, in Italian and English, and his especial favourite, Sir Walter Raleigh's *History of the World*. He had bought this when he was still a schoolboy in Glasgow and was so unwilling to be separated from it that, when his things were packed up for the move to St Andrews, he himself carried the precious ponderous volume all the way.

Of all the Latin poets, his favourite was Lucan, with his vigorous, vivid descriptions of Pompey and Caesar at war. Sometimes he made poetry himself. On the fly-leaf of his *Caesar* he wrote in his bold, flowing hand:

> *If Caesar's paragon I cannot be*
> *Yet shall I soar in thoughts as high as he.*

The story of Alexander the Great stirred his admiration. All his life his thoughts would return in wonder to the amazing son of Philip of Macedon who, with such small forces and so great a genius, had defeated the great King of the Persians. This time he wrote on the fly-leaf of the book:

> *As Philip's noble son did still disdain*
> *All but the dear applause of merited fame,*
> *And nothing harboured in that lofty brain*
> *But how to conquer an eternal name:*
> *So, great attempts, heroic ventures shall*
> *Advance my fortune, or renown my fall.*

Montrose at seventeen was ambitious for honour and glory, intelligent, active, generous, popular and handsome. Critical observers noticed that he was also vain. He was fastidious and elegant in his dress and he was proud of his lustrous auburn hair which curled naturally into the fashionable lovelocks of the time. Very sure of his own opinions, he was inclined to think poorly of anyone who disagreed with him; it was a fault which sometimes made him enemies.

He could hardly help being vain. He had been born, the only son and heir to the Earl of Montrose, after his mother had prayed and waited twenty years for a boy. From childhood he had been surrounded by affectionate sisters and admiring relations. When he succeeded his father as Earl of Montrose, at the age of fourteen, a council of nine guardians had been appointed to look after him. They were his cousins, the heads of the various junior branches of the great family of Graham, or his brothers-in-law. His favourite was his eldest sister's husband, Lord Napier, whom he regarded almost as a father, but he got on pretty well with them all. At home, at school, at the University, he had all his heart could desire – a sword of precious Italian workmanship, a cross-bow inlaid with mother-of-pearl, gilded spurs, rich clothes and 'mettled hound and managed hawk and palfry fresh and fair'. Even his arrows were brought from London because London arrows were regarded as the best. He grew up rich, handsome, healthy, beloved, a spoilt child of fortune.

It says much for his character that he did not grow up selfish, arrogant and wilful; on the contrary. Both as a boy and in after life he liked to have his own way and was always a little surprised when he did not get it; yet all accounts agree that he was good tempered and sweet natured, a kind master and a loyal friend. His ideal of noble conduct was founded on the romantic tales of chivalry that he loved – on the valiant Crusaders and faithful lovers of Tasso's poem. He believed in loyalty, truth and honour, in generosity to a defeated foe and the

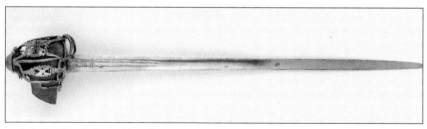

A basket-handled sword by John Simpson which carries Montrose's coat of arms (Glasgow Museums: Art Gallery and Museum, Kelvingrove)

protection of the weak. One of his critics was later to say that he 'lived as in a romance'. But romance alone cannot form a character and he owed as much, or more, to the stern Protestant religion in which, like the majority of his fellow Scots, he had been carefully instructed. Time was to show that the gay and chivalrous Montrose had an iron strength.

Montrose came of a family distinguished for loyalty and courage. In the fourteenth century Sir John Graham had been the devoted friend and lieutenant of Sir William Wallace in the struggle against the English. His descendants, the Earls of Montrose, had made it their honourable tradition to support the Crown in the civil wars which so often afflicted Scotland.

They had another tradition as well. Their lands, scattered in an irregular triangle with its base running from the seaport of Montrose to the Ochill hills and its apex beyond Stirling, lay like a narrowing wedge across the heart of Scotland, between the Anglo-Saxon English-speaking lowlands (to which the Grahams themselves truly belonged) and the Gaelic-speaking Celtic Highlands. In the past they, with the other landowners of this district, had been responsible for holding back the wild Highlandmen from raiding the fertile lowlands. Their principal castle, Kincardine on the flank of the Ochills, had been built for watch and ward against such raids.

Scotland's elder statesmen looked with a friendly eye on the hopeful boy. The Chancellor asked him to dinner, and the Archbishop had him to stay. Both were impressed by his intelligence and charm. He could suit his conversation and manner to the gravity of such visits, but his tearing spirits needed other outlets. The weeks after he left St Andrews found him at one moment hunting on the shores of Loch Lomond, at another displaying his prowess as an archer to the good people of his own town of Montrose, or playing golf, or receiving the freedom of the city at Aberdeen with great feasting and ringing of bells. Everywhere he went money slid through his fingers.

'To the poor at the gate 2/–

To the poor at the Kirk 4/–

To a dwarf begging from my Lord at his Chamber door 18/–

To a boy who brought some trout 8/–

To some more poor 2/–. . . . '

So the accounts run on, carefully kept by a conscientious steward. Thrift was not one of the young lord's virtues.

In between the hunting and the shooting and the visiting of that autumn after he left the University, Montrose spent a week at Kinnaird Castle, the seat of a neighbouring nobleman, Lord Carnegie. Here in the presence of his guardians he signed a marriage contract and, on the following day, took to wife Lord Carnegie's sixth and youngest daughter, Magdalen. She was about his own age and even in those days of early marriages, Montrose and his wife were thought to be too young to set up house together. For the next years she continued to live at Kinnaird with her parents, and he lived at Kinnaird as much as he lived anywhere. But he was never in one place for long. Restless, active, popular, he rode from

Kinnaird Castle as it looks today. This is where Montrose married Magdalen, daughter of Lord Carnegie (Royal Commission on the Ancient and Historical Monuments of Scotland)

Tom Sydserf by Michael Wright (Private Collection)

one friendly house to another, a gay and welcome guest; he went hunting the deer and walking over the hills until he knew the passes and ranges, the moors and gorges and glens as well as any man in Scotland.

A nobleman's education was not complete until he had seen

something more than his native land. At twenty, therefore, he took leave of his stay-at-home wife and the two little sons already born to them, and set out to see the sights of Europe.

He did not go alone. That, for a young nobleman in the seventeenth century, would have been thought unsuitable. A valet, a couple of grooms, two or more pages would be essential, as also a trusted servant to look after the money bag and chaffer with the innkeepers, and a major-domo or steward to keep all the others in order. Montrose's travelling party seems to have included, in various capacities, several of his own kinsmen, as well as a young friend called Tom Sydserf. His father was a reverend clergyman and a scholar, but Tom was made of brisker stuff. He was in the course of his long life to be poet, soldier, journalist, scout, spy, and finally actor-manager of the first theatrical company to be established in Edinburgh. At this time he was a gay young man fresh from college, with quick wits and a ready interest in everything. He got on famously with Montrose; the friendship was to last.

The first winter was spent in France at Angers, where Montrose studied the art of war among the young French nobles at the most famous military college in Europe. France, under the firm, despotic guidance of Cardinal Richelieu, was a country rising rapidly to triumphant greatness. Paris, which Montrose often visited, was growing under the very eyes of travellers. The old muddy streets were being paved and widened. Noble churches and spacious squares were being built. A young man, sensitive to beauty, who had seen nothing grander than the high dark streets of Edinburgh, must have looked with pleasure and surprise at the pretty new Place Royale with its green-shuttered houses of pink brick and the broad arcade over the pavement to shelter the citizens from the rain. How graceful, in his eyes, must have seemed the garlanded façades of the new houses and churches after the angular gothic and forbidding granite of Scotland.

Montrose spent a year in France. Then he went on to Italy, to see the coloured cities with their cathedrals of striped marble, the glowing mosaics and venerable ruins, the picture galleries, the huge modern churches and the abundant treasures of Rome. He would have liked to go yet farther afield and had plans for proceeding to Turkey, to see for himself the curiosities which he knew from the account of his writer protégé, William Lithgow. But insistent messages from his friends and family in Scotland called him home. He had been abroad for three years. It was high time for him to come back to his wife and his lands. It was high time, too, for him to perform another essential duty.

In all his travels Montrose had not yet visited the English Court. He had not kissed the hand of his sovereign lord, King Charles. This delay in performing the necessary courtesy of a distinguished subject to his king needs some explanation.

The answer cannot be found without going back into the past. Nine years before Montrose had been born, King James VI of Scots had become King of England. Before he hurried off to his richer, southern kingdom he had promised to come back every third year to his native land. Yet only once, after fifteen years' absence, had he done so. His son, King Charles, born in Scotland, had been brought up in England from childhood. He had succeeded to his father's throne in 1625, but he had let eight years go by before he took the road to the north, to be crowned King of Scots.

The Scots felt deeply, but differently, about this neglect. Some thought the king had acted wisely in going to the softer, easier, richer country. They followed his example, and flocked southward to grow rich on his bounty. The old king liked to hear Scots voices round him and to see faces he had known when he was young. The new king had been brought up among these men and their sons. He, too, surrounded himself with them and gave them places of power and trust. These men were not much liked in England; in Scotland they were hated. The Scots are a proud people; *fier comme un Ecossois* – 'as proud as a Scot' – went the French proverb. But the Scots who had hurried after their king to eat greedily of the English fleshpots were not proud, and the Scots who stayed behind despised them as time-servers who had

lowered the honour of Scotland for the sake of
English gold.

Among these who stayed in Scotland there
were two ways of thinking. The bold,
ambitious and unscrupulous rejoiced because
there was now no king to check them. But the
majority of honest men, noble or simple,
regretted and resented the king's absence. They
regretted it for their country's sake, feeling that
Scotland was slighted. They resented it for their
own sakes because the Court, the centre for
their honourable ambition, had been removed
too far away.

*Charles I by Sir Robert Strange after
Van Dyck (National Galleries of
Scotland)*

If Montrose thought of the matter at all in
his happy, active youth, he felt in this last way
about it. This may have been the reason that he
had taken so little trouble to make himself
known to the king.

Of all the absentee Scots the one least loved in Scotland and in
England, was James, Marquess of Hamilton. Of all the absentee Scots he
was most beloved of the king. Charles, who was shy and had a slight
stammer, found the arrogant manner and pompous wordy speech of
Hamilton strangely attractive. But the bold and fluent favourite was also
conceited, obstinate, jealous, ambitious, unscrupulous and deceitful.

When Hamilton heard that Montrose was in London he took steps
to see that this accomplished young man should be prevented from
becoming a rival at Court. First he saw Montrose and told him
untruthfully that the king did not like Scots; he cared only for England
and the English. Then he sought out the king, and reported that
Montrose was an over-confident, ambitious young man to whom His
Majesty would be well advised to pay as little attention as possible.

Hamilton's plan succeeded beyond expectation. Montrose, already

James, Marquess and later 1st Duke of Hamilton, by an unknown artist after Van Dyck
(National Galleries of Scotland)

warned that the king despised the Scots, did not expect a warm reception. But he could hardly fail to be hurt when Charles casually extended his hand to be kissed, without a word, and almost without looking at the ardent young stranger at his feet, drew it quickly back and turned away. For perhaps the first time in his twenty-four years Montrose had been slighted.

This was his only meeting with King Charles before that great storm broke over the unhappy monarch's head, in which he himself and so many of his subjects lost their lives.

Already there were faint rumblings of trouble to come. Montrose, in London, must have heard them. Sydserf, his steward, was the son of a learned clergyman who had lately been made Bishop of Orkney. Bishop Sydserf, well pleased with his new dignity, was in London at this time, bustling in and out of Lambeth Palace with half a dozen other Scots bishops having long conferences with the Archbishop of Canterbury, William Laud.

It is reasonable to suppose that Tom Sydserf, when he reached London, sought out his father to tell him of his adventures abroad. It is not unreasonable to guess that Montrose, too, visited the good bishop, that all three dined and talked together more than once. Bishop Sydserf made no secret of what he was doing in London. He and his fellow Scots bishops were composing a new Prayer Book, very similar to the English one, which the king desired should be used in Scotland.

Montrose had much to think of when he set out on the last part of his journey home: the great power of Hamilton at Court, the cold behaviour of the king, and the disturbing knowledge that, in Lambeth Palace by London, a new Prayer Book was being drawn up for compulsory use in Scotland.

CHAPTER TWO

FOR GOD, COVENANT AND COUNTRY

After his long minority and his long absence, Montrose now brought his wife, Magdalen, home to his own house and lands. They lived partly at Kincardine, the grey castle in the shelter of the Ochill hills where he had spent his childhood, and partly in a more spacious modern house at the seaport of old Montrose. Two children, John and James, had been born before he went on his travels. In time there were three more, David (who died young), Robert and Jean. There were happy times at Montrose and Kincardine Castle in the few years before civil war divided Scotland. There were hunting parties and shooting parties, and in the long winter evenings music and singing and dancing. The hungry poet, Lithgow, mindful of the help he had been given in the past, came to share in the hospitality of Montrose's table. Scotland's greatest living writer, Drummond of Hawthornden, rode over from time to time to talk of politics or poetry.

For five or six years the large stone house on the windy coast and the sheltered castle under the flank of the hills made a peaceful background to Montrose's life. But his active mind was not made for a tranquil existence, and within six months of his home-coming he was involved in the political struggle from which he was never again to escape.

The new Prayer Book, of which he had heard in London, had now been printed in Scotland. Rather oddly for a book devoted to the worship of God, it began with a threat from the king. Any minister of religion who did not use this book – so ran the notice on the title page – would be declared a rebel. The threat did not please the proud Scots.

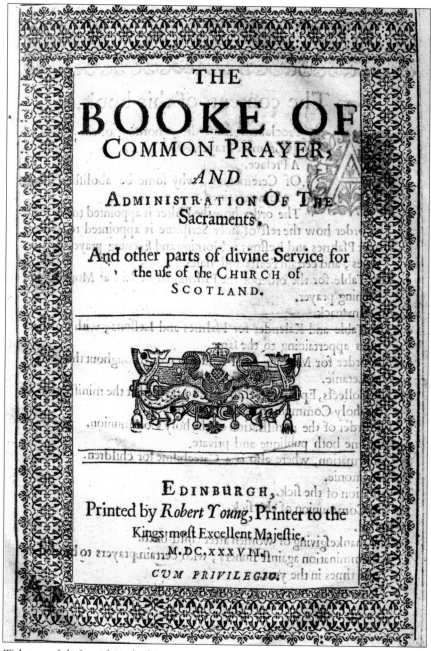

Title page of the Scottish Book of Common Prayer, 1627 (The Trustees of the National Library of Scotland)

Many, who might otherwise have accepted the Book, set their faces against it because of the manner in which it was forced upon them. Many more opposed it for deeper reasons. The majority of Scots preferred a simpler service with extempore prayers to the set words and set answers of the Prayer Book. There were other things, too, which they did not like. The use of the cross in baptism and the proposed order of Holy Communion appeared to them too much like the Church of Rome.

On Sunday 23 July 1637, when the new Book was to be used for the first time, a distinguished congregation met in the great Church of St Giles in Edinburgh. The King's Councillors, the Judges, the Archbishop of St Andrews and the Bishop of Edinburgh were ranged in the places of honour; ladies and gentlemen of rank filled the body of the church. Below them crowded the waiting maids, the serving men and the good citizens of Edinburgh. As soon as the Dean began to read,

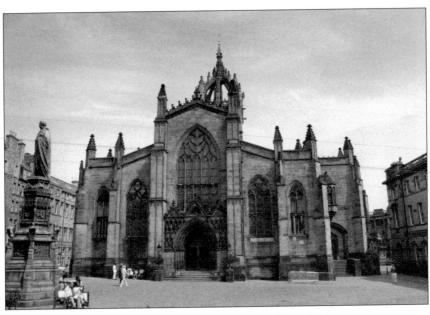

St Giles' Church, Edinburgh (Richard Foulsham)

these raised their voices in a hubbub of protest. The Bishop of Edinburgh stepped boldly into the pulpit and ordered them to be quiet. The only answer was a folding stool sent hurtling at his head by a vigorous female hand. It was followed by a hailstorm of folding stools and clasp bibles.

Scenes of the same kind were happening all over Scotland. Few ministers tried to read the service, and of those who tried fewer still were allowed to finish by their congregations. At Brechin Cathedral, just by Kinnaird, Bishop Whitford managed to read the Book without interruption, but then he took the precaution of placing two loaded pistols squarely in sight of all on the crimson pulpit cushions in front of him.

When the king and Court at Whitehall heard how the Scots had received the new Book, the king's Scots jester, Archie Armstrong, came capering up to the Archbishop in triumph. 'Wha's feule now?' he asked. Charles dismissed him on the spot and ordered his Council in Scotland to enforce the use of the new Prayer Book with all the rigour of the law. When the king's orders were read out in Council, some of those who heard them shook their heads and others shook in their shoes. The Council could as soon control the raging sea as the Edinburgh mob. Half the country was in uproar. From parish after parish petitions flowed in denouncing 'the English Popish Mass Service Book'.

The opposition soon found a leader in the jolly, red-faced Earl of Rothes, who rode from one great house to another in the long days of the late summer talking and persuading. At one time or another, and perhaps more than once, he and his cavalcade must have come clattering into the courtyard of Kincardine Castle to drink a cup of wine or stay for a night's lodging with Montrose and his lady.

Loyalty to the Crown was an unbroken tradition in the Graham family. So was loyalty to the freedom of Scotland. In the great hall at Kincardine hung the antique sword, revered as that of Sir John

John Leslie, 6th Earl of Rothes, by George Jamesone (Private Collection)

Graham who had fought with Wallace. Montrose's great-grandfather had been killed fighting the English invader at Pinkie, and his great-great-grandfather at Flodden. But where lay the loyalty of a true Scot when Scotland's king had become England's king and from the safety, strength and distance of England sought to change the religion of Scotland? It was not an easy question for an honest man to answer.

Montrose did not hesitate long. He did not look upon the opposition to his Prayer Book as rebellion against the king, but rather as a necessary protest to which the king would listen if he were wise. By the autumn he had openly taken his place with Rothes among the leaders of that protest.

Three months later, in Edinburgh, on 20 February 1638 the royal heralds, to the sound of trumpets, once again proclaimed king Charles's will from the Market Cross; the Prayer Book was to be used in Scotland, whether the Scots would or no.

The dignity of the occasion was somewhat marred because Rothes and his friends had taken up their station on a specially constructed platform immediately next to the Market Cross whence they defiantly watched the proceedings. As soon as the king's heralds had finished, out spoke Rothes in protest. He was followed by Montrose, who, in order to be heard and seen the better by the people, up-ended an empty barrel left conveniently lying on the scaffold, and climbed on top of it; 'James,' Rothes reproached him, smiling, 'you will not be at rest till you be lifted up there above the rest in three fathom of rope.'

A week later, led by Rothes and Montrose, a huge crowd met in Grey Friars Churchyard, under the frowning eminence of Edinburgh Castle.

There they unrolled the great parchment which was to become known as the National Covenant. It is a lengthy statement, tracing the history of the Reformation in Scotland and repeating the substance of certain earlier declarations of the Scottish faith, but it concludes with a nobly defiant promise – 'From the knowledge and conscience of our duty to God, to our king and country, without any worldly respect or inducement, we promise and swear by the great name of the Lord our God to continue in the profession and obedience of the aforesaid religion; that we shall defend the same, and resist all those contrary errors and corruptions according to our vocation, and to the utmost of that power that God hath put into our hands, all the days of our life.' They spread the Covenant out flat, on a tombstone for a table, and for three days, wet or fine, from morn to dusk, the scratching of the pen never ceased.

A dozen copies of the Covenant were made and carried from one town to the next. From far and wide men came to set their names to it with prayers and tears of thanksgiving. 'I have seen more than a thousand persons all at once,' wrote a minister in his diary, 'holding up their hands and the tears falling down from their eyes.' It was a grave and solemn thing that had happened, this defiance of the king for conscience' sake, and not in Scotland only. By many an English fireside, in many an English home, men and women held up their hands to heaven with the tears falling down from their eyes in thanksgiving for what the Scots had done.

The reason for this uprising of the Scots and the surge of sympathy which swept the English must be sought in the past. A hundred years before, when the Reformation had destroyed the unity of Catholic Christendom, Scotland and England had alike abandoned the old religion. In England the Anglican settlement had been reached under Queen Elizabeth, while in Scotland Calvinism had triumphed.

The Anglican Church repudiated the authority of the Pope but retained the archbishops and bishops of the Catholic hierarchy and established a set order of public worship. A considerable party in

19

England, loosely called the Puritans, considered this reformation inadequate and clamoured for the more extreme Protestantism of John Calvin as practised at Geneva.

Calvin's doctrines, contained in the thousand pages of his *Institutes*, cannot be easily reduced to a few sentences. Briefly, he argued thus: God exists for all time and from all time. Past, present and future are alike comprehended in his infinite Now. It is therefore impossible for any human being to do anything that God has not already foreseen. Calvin linked this doctrine of Predestination with his equally important doctrine of Grace. Every Christian knows that Christ died that our sins may be forgiven, in the religious phrase, that we may have Grace. Most Churches hold that a man will in the course of his life sometimes be 'in a state of Grace' and sometimes not; a bad man forfeits his right to God's pardon, but he may regain it by repentance. Without Grace there is no salvation.

But if, as Calvin held, God foreknows all that a man will do before that man is born, then God must also know whether at the last he will prove worthy of Grace. Calvin therefore taught that every man is born with or without Grace; in other words, that he is damned or saved to all eternity before he is born.

This hard but logical belief created an iron obstinacy and strength of will among those who held it. They conceived themselves at least in some measure able to judge who, among the living, were the saved and who the damned. Among the best, this conviction of being the Elect produced a noble courage and exaltation; among the worst, a vindictive self-righteousness.

Apart from these profound beliefs, the English Calvinists wished the Anglican Church to abandon its bishops, its vestments and its set order of worship. They would have liked to see it governed with the help of lay elders as was Calvin's Church at Geneva and the other Calvinist churches abroad; they would have liked extempore prayers and more preaching and expounding of the Scriptures than the Anglicans encouraged. In the face of criticism, the Anglican Church struck back, suppressed Puritan preachers, broke up their conventicles, prosecuted the writers of Puritan books. These stubborn persecuted people therefore, all over England, turned with hearts full of hope and gratitude to the Covenanters in Scotland.

In Scotland, during the troubles of the Reformation, Calvinism, under the formidable leadership of John Knox, had swept the country. The old religion lingered in parts of the Highlands or here and there in regions protected by some great man who remained loyal to it. But Calvinism, under the more familiar name of Presbyterianism, was the dominant religion of the country. After the death of Knox the first enthusiasm slackened, and King James VI, who saw in the growing authority of ministers a threat to his own, managed by diplomacy and pressure to impose archbishops and bishops on the Scots Kirk. They were by no means popular with the people, but they had managed more or less to retain their uneasy position until Charles I, in an evil hour, set out to complete the work begun by his father, and to bring the Kirk into line with the English Church.

The Service Book was not the only change he had in mind. At the Reformation much Church land had been seized by rapacious lords and Charles was anxious to regain from their descendants the estates which had once belonged to the Scots bishoprics. Among those who opposed the king's projected plans for the Kirk there was a growing number of men whose anxieties were rather for their property than for freedom of conscience. The power and influence of these men among their tenantry was not without effect in giving to the Covenanting party in Scotland its increasingly formidable strength.

Taken by surprise, the king played for time. He even made an apparent concession. He gave permission for the Assembly of the Scots Kirk to meet. What he gave with one hand, however, he made ready to take with the other, for he appointed the Marquess of Hamilton to preside over the deliberations, and instructed him to dissolve the Assembly at the first sign of opposition.

The Assembly met in Glasgow in the autumn of 1638. They elected as their moderator or chairman, Alexander Henderson, a wise and far-seeing minister who had had a great hand in drafting the Covenant. Next, they protested against the new Prayer Book. Hamilton immediately closed the session, or rather he tried to do so. He rose in his stately fashion and stalked out of the hall with all the members of the King's Council, except one, obediently following. No one else left and the meeting went on.

Next day he dissolved the Assembly by proclamation on pain of treason. Still it sat on. It rejected the new Prayer Book; it abolished archbishops and bishops; it declared null and void the acts of the Assemblies which had met under king James VI; it appointed a commission to inquire into the conduct of ministers. Having thus triumphantly asserted the right of the Scots Kirk to govern itself, it broke up with a resolution to meet again next year.

While these great things were doing, Lord Lorne, who alone of the King's Council had stayed when Hamilton left, had unobtrusively arrogated to himself the place that Hamilton had left vacant. This renegade member of the King's Council, who had not, when the Assembly met, so much as signed the Covenant, now took to himself a higher place than all the other Scots lords who had worked for the Covenant for the past year.

His full name was Archibald Campbell, Viscount Lorne, and he was eldest son to the Earl of Argyll. But he already possessed all his father's lands for the old earl had forfeited them when he became a Roman Catholic. The old earl lived in London and was still received at Court by the king. On one occasion he had solemnly warned His Majesty against his son; 'he will wind you a pirn,' he said in the homely Scots phrase, meaning he will make trouble for you.

The personal appearance of Lord Lorne was against him. He was a small, lean, red-haired man, with thin, bloodless lips, and a squint which gave an unattractive leering look to his already plain face. But

Alexander Henderson, attributed to Van Dyck (National Galleries of Scotland)

he was immensely powerful. He owned a great part of the south-western Highlands, and by advancing money to poorer or less provident lords he had gained indirect control over yet wider lands. The Marquess of Huntly, for instance, was deeply in his debt.

Lorne was something more than a great noble; he was also among the most powerful of the Highland chiefs, being the head of the large and wealthy Campbell clan. His people's primitive urge for expansion at the expense of their neighbours served at one and the same time as an excuse and a weapon for the acquisitive policy of their chief. The Campbells had already overwhelmed the MacGregors, and they were in the process of overwhelming the Macdonalds.

It was this latter rivalry, the embittered feud of Macdonald and Campbell, which now began to exert its influence on the broader politics of Scotland. The Macdonalds were a widely scattered clan with lands not only in the western Highlands and Isles but also in northern Ireland. They had at this time no very remarkable Scots chieftain, but the chief of the Irish clan was of some importance. He was Randal Macdonnell (so the Irish spelt the name) Earl of Antrim, and he had been brought up from boyhood at the Court of Charles I. Here he had grown into a silly, handsome young gallant with every qualification for a man about town and none for a Highland chief. But he felt for the wrongs of his people because, among other things, they affected his purse. Furthermore, he was a great favourite with Archbishop Laud and had consolidated his position with the king by marrying, as her second husband, the buxom widow of the murdered favourite, the Great Duke of Buckingham. With support such as this he had had no difficulty in persuading the king to grant back to him a wide stretch of land in Scotland – no less than the whole district of Kintyre, which had been occupied by the Campbells for the past thirty years.

Lord Lorne's decision to join the Covenanters looked suspiciously as though it were connected with this ill-considered grant of the king's. Certainly his change of sides was followed immediately by the marshalling of Campbell troops in the threatened province of Kintyre.

Since the Assembly had defied him, King Charles had determined to reduce the Scots by force. He now called on the lords and gentry of England to appear at York in April 1639, each with his proper contingent of soldiers. The Covenanters took up the challenge. Over all the south of Scotland that spring men left the plough to take up arms; they might be seen in every town and village learning the use of pike and musket.

Scotland had been at peace for over fifty years, yet many professional soldiers stiffened the Covenanting army. In those times when it was usual for governments to employ hired professional soldiers to fight their wars, adventurous Scots often sought their fortunes on the battlefields of Europe. Many of these now hurried home to instruct the new recruits. Chief among them was a distinguished veteran of Gustavus Adolphus's army, Alexander Leslie, who was appointed commander-in-chief. But a high command, by common consent, went to the young Montrose.

Meanwhile, the English armed unwillingly at their king's bidding. Sympathy with the Scots and dislike of the unnecessary war was the prevailing sentiment. The most serious threat to the Covenanters lay not in the half-hearted English preparations but within Scotland itself. The region north and west of Aberdeen, in which the Gordons predominated, began to stir against the Covenant. The religion of the Marquess of Huntly, chief of the Gordons, was doubtful; he was a very dubious Catholic if a Catholic at all, but many of his clan were loyal to

General Alexander Leslie, 1st Earl of Leven, attributed to George Jamesone (National Galleries of Scotland)

George Gordon, 1st Marquess of Huntly and his wife (National Galleries of Scotland)

the old religion and whatever he was himself he was certainly not a Calvinist. A delegation of Covenanters, led by Montrose in person, had tried to bring the district in to sign the Covenant in the previous summer but had met with very moderate success.

Huntly now declared for the king, and began to gather his clan. Montrose, with a band of picked musketeers, made a lightning march across the hills, and stationed himself at the little village of Turriff, Huntly's rendezvous. This unexpected intrusion sufficiently unnerved Huntly, who first altered the place of his rendezvous and then made personal overtures to Montrose.

As one Scots lord to another, he suggested that each of them should undertake to remain in his own territory for the duration of hostilities. But Montrose was not in a position to negotiate as one Scots lord with another; he was Leslie's second in command and Leslie had decided that, to secure the rear of the Covenanting army, the city of Aberdeen must be occupied before the main body of the army marched to defend the Border against King Charles.

Huntly's messengers came gloomily home to their chief. It was a raw March day and they saw the sun rise, a dark and angry red, the colour of blood fresh spilt in a silver dish, they thought, and shook their heads at the omen.

Huntly Castle has a frieze dated 1602 which commemorates the 1st Marquess of Huntly and his wife (Jim Henderson)

Yet March went out in a spell of gay and brilliant weather. It was under blue skies, in bright sunlight, that Montrose's army marched on Aberdeen. At their head floated his banner of blue silk on which were painted in letters of gold 'For God, Covenant and Country'. He provided every man in his forces with a length of bright blue silk ribbon. The infantry twisted them into cockades and stuck them in their bonnets; the cavalry wore them slung from shoulder to hip as scarves. The more solemn ministers referred sourly to this frivolous adornment as 'Montrose's whimsy'. But the gay ribbons served a useful purpose, in a time when uniforms were unknown, in marking out the troops of the Covenant.

Huntly, in his usual state of indecision, disbanded his clan. It seemed too good to be true. 'The wicked flee while no man pursueth' quoted the ministers as they marched into Aberdeen.

Their entry was at first orderly and peaceful. Montrose had given his word that no one should suffer and that all provisions would be paid for. Leslie, however, trained in the savage German wars, was less scrupulous. There was a violent-sounding German word often on the lips of the soldiers who had served abroad – *Plunder*. This was not robbery for which a man could be hanged, but licensed theft, the soldiers' immemorial right. With Leslie's approval the plundering soon began. On that day the ugly foreign word became a part of the English language.

Montrose tried to mend matters by taking some of the citizens under his personal protection. His interference was bitterly resented, and most of all, to his distress, by some of the ministers who had come with the army. They wanted to smite the Aberdonians as the children of Israel had smitten the Amalekites.

This first shock was followed by a second. Montrose had taken the occasion to seek out Huntly. In a long friendly talk he had persuaded him – it was something of a diplomatic triumph – to sign the Covenant. Huntly made two reservations: he reserved his loyalty to the king and the right of his clan to their own religion. Montrose had gained the essential point – Huntly's neutrality for the rest of the war.

Pleased with his achievement he invited Huntly to Aberdeen to ratify the agreement, pledging his word that no harm should befall him. But when he reached Aberdeen with his distinguished guest he found that his colleagues looked upon the matter in a different light. In vain he pleaded that he had given his word of honour to Huntly. He was overruled and outvoted. Huntly and his eldest son were sent as prisoners to Edinburgh. It was a betrayal for which Huntly never forgave Montrose.

Montrose had acted unwisely in pledging his word without being sure that he could keep it. But he had acted far more wisely than his allies when he sought to neutralize rather than to capture Huntly. The Gordons, outraged at the seizure of their chief, now sprang to arms, and the Gordons, deprived of the vacillating Huntly, were far more formidable than they had been before. Montrose and Leslie had no

The Old Bridge of Dee, where the battle of the same name was fought in 1639
(Jim Henderson)

sooner marched for the Border than they surged into Aberdeen and expelled the garrison. Montrose came back and retook the town, but now Huntly's second son, Lord Aboyne, appeared off the coast with ships borrowed from the king's fleet, and Montrose withdrew to meet the reinforcements on their way to his help under Colonel Middleton. So came about the first serious encounter of the Civil Wars, when Montrose and Middleton, for two long summer days, battered Aboyne and the Gordons out of Aberdeen. The battle is known to history as Brig o' Dee from the high stone bridge over the river where the fighting was hottest.

On 23 June 1639 the Covenanting army entered Aberdeen for the third time, and for the third time Montrose, in spite of the grumbling

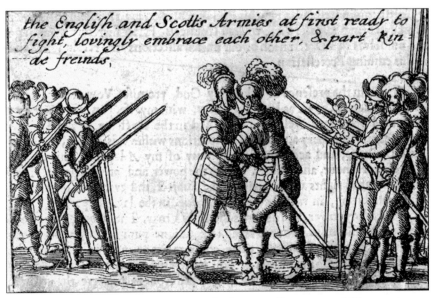

the English and Scotts Armies at first ready to fight, lovingly embrace each other, & part kinde freinds,

The Pacification of Berwick was used by Charles as a stalling measure. This engraving, c. 1639 presents the Parliamentarian view of the event (Ashmolean Museum, Oxford)

of his troops and the black looks of some of the ministers, forbade them to sack the town.

On that same day, on the Border, king Charles had patched up a temporary peace. When he reached the Tweed with his discontented English troops, he had only to look across at Leslie's well-ordered army to see that this was no time for him to fight.

Montrose got the news a few days later and at once disbanded his forces. That summer's campaigning had revealed something of the military gifts – the speed, decision and judgement – which were to make him famous. It had also shown him that many who fought for the Covenant fell short of his standards of honour, mercy and justice. Yet more unwelcome shocks awaited him during the winter's peace which succeeded that summer's war.

CHAPTER THREE

KING CHARLES OR
KING CAMPBELL?

By the Pacification of Berwick King Charles agreed to call a free Assembly of the Kirk and a free Parliament in Scotland. As soon as peace was signed General Leslie asked him to visit the Covenanting camp and review the troops. As he rode along their ranks, they threw up their blue-cockaded bonnets and cheered him loudly. 'God bless His Majesty,' they cried, 'and the Devil confound the Bishops.' Charles was not pleased.

Soon afterwards he gave orders that the bishops were to attend the coming Assembly. His luckless councillors in Edinburgh, who had to make this unwelcome announcement, suffered for it. Two of them were set on by the mob, from whose clutches they escaped with difficulty and without some of their clothes. Rothes, taking with him Montrose and some other lords, hastened to Berwick to expostulate with the king. Charles received them coolly and, playing for time, told them to go back to Edinburgh and fetch the rest of the Covenanting lords.

This command set the Scots lords thinking. If they fetched their friends and came back to Berwick, would they be seized and carried prisoners to London? They decided not to take the risk, and made it clear, in the excuse that they sent to the king, that they feared a trap. He returned the terse answer that if they would not trust themselves with him, he would not trust himself with them. He went back to London and left Hamilton to open Parliament in Edinburgh. This was the final blow to the unstable peace which had been signed at Berwick.

Berwick in the early seventeenth century, from the town plan by John Speed

The Assembly – without the bishops – met in Edinburgh in no very good humour. First it confirmed the abolition of Episcopacy, then it declared that the signing of the Covenant was to be made compulsory throughout Scotland, and finally it excommunicated several eminent Royalists and a number of ministers who had opposed the Covenant.

A spirit of vindictive intolerance was growing among the victorious Covenanters. The jovial good humour of Rothes, the chivalry of Montrose, even the wise moderation of such ministers as Alexander Henderson were out of favour. Henderson, it is true, maintained his position and prestige among them, but in general the ministers who now rose to the fore were more bitter and more violent. Already the evil custom was spreading of using religious sanctions for political ends. Exclusion from the congregation and from the Lord's Table – as they called the Communion service – was a useful coercive weapon against their opponents.

To an honest but not bigoted Calvinist like Montrose this was a rank abuse of religion. He disliked the developments in the Kirk all the more because this violent party among the ministers seemed to be, wittingly or unwittingly, wedded to a political faction which he distrusted. The popular fervour which had given birth to the Covenant was now being artificially stimulated by organized mob violence, intimidation and force. In Montrose's own words, those who had 'found the sweetness of government' were principally concerned only to maintain their new power.

The faction was led by Lord Lorne, now Earl of Argyll, with the help of Archibald Johnstone of Warristoun, a singularly able lawyer, but in other ways a brain-sick and bitter neurotic. It had gained mastery over the Scots Parliament. The method used was simple, for the Scots Parliament acted, not like the English Parliament as a body of individuals, but through a committee called the Lords of the Articles or more familiarly the Committee of Estates. Of recent years this committee had frequently been 'packed' in the king's interests. But Argyll now introduced legislation to prevent this.

Montrose, vehemently but in vain, opposed this legislation on the grounds that it trenched too far on the royal authority and might lead to the exploitation of Parliament by factions. His anxieties, at least as to the king's position, were justified when Parliament, now almost wholly under the domination of Argyll, reassembled in the following June in open defiance of a prohibition from the king. Scots affairs, under the leadership of Argyll, were taking what seemed to him a very ugly turn.

It will be seen from this that Argyll, with ten years' experience on the King's Council, was a wily political strategist. Montrose, at twenty-eight, with no experience of political intrigue and a naturally frank nature, was not likely to be a match for him. Yet it became increasingly clear, when death removed Rothes from the scene, that if there was to be any moderate party, opposed to the extremists among the Covenanters, Montrose was its natural leader. He had already

Archibald Campbell, 1st Marquess of Argyll, by David Scougall
(National Galleries of Scotland)

drawn attention to himself by opposing Argyll in Parliament and by protesting against the victimization of the defeated.

The chief advantage that Montrose enjoyed was his easy popularity with the people. His enemies, therefore, set out to undermine their trust in him. They put it about that the king had won him over when he saw him at Berwick. An unknown hand pinned a paper on the door of his lodging in Edinburgh. '*Invictus armis, verbis vincitur,*' it read, and the learned who jostled up to read it construed it for the unlearned: 'Unconquered in arms, he was conquered by words.'

The ingenious slander was widely believed. It did its deadly work against Montrose's reputation not only among contemporaries; it has found its way into many later accounts of his career. Yet the facts speak loud against it. Montrose had only seen the king briefly at Berwick, in company with other lords, and Charles had made no attempt to win him over. Whatever Montrose's feelings towards the faction in power, he remained wholly faithful to the Covenant, in letter and in spirit.

But now Argyll made a move which roused Montrose to action. Ostensibly in the interests of the Covenant, he invaded and laid waste the lands of the Ogilvies. The Ogilvies were for the most part against the Covenant, but they were near neighbours of Montrose (their chief, Lord Airlie, was his first cousin), and he had himself taken order with them. They had given up their arms and accepted token garrisons from him. By no stretch of imagination could it be argued that, thus disarmed, they represented any danger to the Covenanting party. Argyll's expedition was a barefaced raid in quest of booty. As such it has been fixed for posterity in a contemporary ballad which is still sung:

> *It fell on a day, and a bonnie summer day,*
> *When green grew oats and barley,*
> *That there fell out a great dispute*
> *Between Argyll and Airlie.*

Lady Ogilvie looks o'er her bower window,
And O but she looks warely!
And there she spied the great Argyll,
Come to plunder the bonnie house of Airlie.

'Come down, come down, my Lady Ogilvie,
Come down and kiss me fairly.'
'O I winna kiss the false Argyll
If he shouldna leave a standing stone in Airlie.'

It was the outrage to the young Lady Ogilvie which had roused the poetic chivalry of the Scots. Argyll had found her alone, defenceless, with a family of little children, had driven her out of her home and burnt it down before her eyes.

Montrose had scarcely digested the shock of this brutal insult to his kinswoman, when he heard rumours of a different and yet more disturbing kind: Argyll had spoken of deposing the king. Given the violent history of Scotland and the not infrequent kidnapping or menacing of monarchs by their over-mighty subjects, the rumour did not sound impossible. In any case, Montrose was not alone in fearing Argyll's ambition. The nickname king Campbell was widely given to him. The king, meanwhile, was preparing for a second attack on Scotland and a project was put forward, ostensibly for the better security of the country, by which Argyll was to be acknowledged virtually as military dictator everywhere north of the Forth. When the scheme was placed before the chief officers of the Scots army Montrose, not without support from others, absolutely refused to concede any such authority to Argyll.

Under the pressure of such events a moderate party was taking shape round Montrose. Chief among his supporters was the wise and cautious Lord Napier, his eldest sister's husband and once his guardian. Some of them met one afternoon in early August at Cumbernauld in

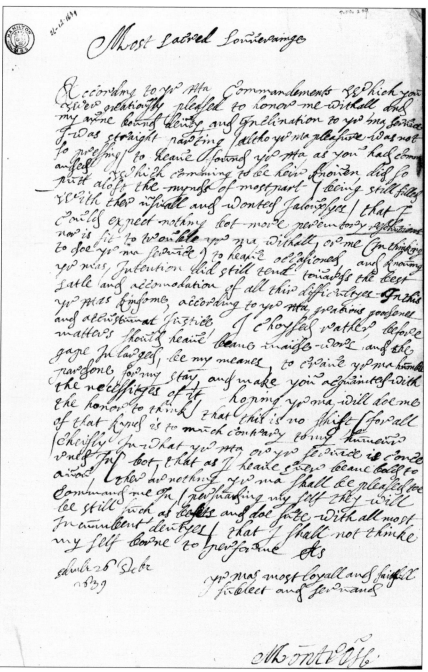

Montrose's letter to Charles I, 26 December 1639, explaining the reasons for his coming to the king (Scottish Record Office, GD406/1/1096)

Sir Archibald Napier, 1st Lord Napier, by George Jamesone, 1637 (National Galleries of Scotland)

Margaret Graham, Lady Napier, wife of the 1st Lord Napier and Montrose's sister, attributed to Adam de Colone, 1626 (National Galleries of Scotland)

Lanarkshire and there, over dinner, drew up and signed a bond, affirming their unswerving intention to defend both king and Covenant against ambitious factions.

But now the king's English army was approaching the Border and political quarrels must take second place until the invaders were repelled. Whatever his doubts of Argyll, Montrose held, with a proud and fatal loyalty, to the Covenant. The Scots had no right to depose their king; but their king had no right to invade them at the head of an English army. So long as Charles stood on the frontiers of Scotland in arms, Montrose would be in arms against him.

The army under the command of Leslie, with Montrose leading a contingent of three thousand horse and foot, reached the Tweed at Coldstream on 20 August 1640. It had been a wet summer and even at the ford the river was full and swift. The honour of leading the vanguard fell to Montrose. Dismounting, he entered the turbulent waters on foot and crossed to the farther bank. But the troops were unwilling to follow the bold example. To encourage his men, he came back and crossed again; this second time they followed him. By nightfall the whole army was over the Tweed.

They passed the ancient, long dismantled bastion of the Roman wall which had held their forefathers at bay. As king James IV had marched, as king David I had marched, they swept into England. The Blue Bonnets were over the Border. The Tyne was the principal line of defence, but their vanguard of a thousand carried the crossing with a rush at Newburn on 27 August. The English fled.

The Scots were well trained, stout hearted and ably led. The English had no spirit for the fight. For the first time in the long quarrelsome history of the two nations, most of them welcomed the Scots invasion. They abandoned Newcastle. The Scots entered in triumph, unresisted. 'Never so many fled from so few,' lamented the king's friends.

King Charles had been beaten, fairly, squarely and surprisingly fast. He had no choice but to offer terms to his rebellious subjects.

It was at this point that Montrose made his first bad mistake in the contest with Argyll. He wrote a private letter to the king, protesting

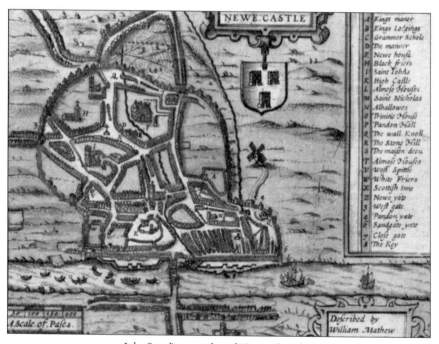

John Speed's town plan of Newcastle, 1610

his loyalty. The letter did not remain a secret. Somehow – and no one quite knows how – it was betrayed. This was the chance for which Argyll had been waiting to undermine Montrose. He was not, as it happened, ignorant of the Cumbernauld Bond and he saw his own way of using it. When challenged, Montrose denied neither the Cumbernauld Bond nor the letter to the king; why should he? He saw nothing wrong in either. But some of the extremists in the party cried out that he and the rest of the 'Bonders' should be tried as traitors for making a division in the party. This did not suit Argyll, for too much might have come out. He persuaded the party to be satisfied for the time being with Montrose's statement that there had been no plot against the Covenant and he asked Montrose to send to Edinburgh all existing copies of the Cumbernauld Bond. The unsuspecting Montrose collected the copies of the document from his friends and handed them over. Thus he placed in his enemies' hands the only written evidence of the truth of his statement that the bond contained no plot against the Covenant. Thereafter hints and lies about its contents were sedulously spread abroad; there was no way in which they could be disproved.

Montrose was slowly learning the skill and ruthlessness of his enemy. The next clash was far more serious. In the summer of 1641 two ministers were hauled up before the Committee of Estates in Edinburgh for having alleged in conversation that Argyll intended the deposition of the king. One of them named Montrose as his source of information.

Montrose was ready for the moment, perhaps even glad of it. It was high time that the truth about Argyll came out. He rose up before the Committee of Estates and declared that John Stewart of Dunkeld had told him that he had heard Argyll, in his tent last July in the braes of Atholl, say that the king should be deposed. John Stewart confirmed his story before the Committee. It was now Argyll's turn to rage. Breaking out into great oaths – an unusual thing with him – he called Stewart a liar. He insisted that he be held for questioning. The luckless man was hurried away to prison. There in the next few days the friends of Argyll saw a good deal of him. They were not violent. They merely pointed out that silly little men ought not to repeat things they had not rightly understood. They confused him with promises of liberty and even of rewards; they hinted dark things of Montrose and Napier. What with confusion, fear and hope, Stewart broke down. His evidence, when brought a second time before the Committee, was not very clear, but it seemed to suggest that Montrose and Napier had set him on to slander Argyll.

John Stewart also informed his questioners that Montrose had recently written to the king by a messenger named Walter Stewart. Walter Stewart was seized on his return. The letter to the king was innocent enough; Montrose had merely sent to Charles some unsolicited and candid advice, urging him to visit Scotland in person and to behave with moderation towards his subjects. There was nothing treasonable, as Charles himself indignantly protested, in a young lord writing to his sovereign. But another paper was found in Walter Stewart's possession which contained some mysterious notes about an elephant and a dromedary. No one has ever unravelled the meaning of this peculiar paper. Montrose himself denied all knowledge of elephants and dromedaries, but the Committee asserted that they were code names and that Montrose had been in a plot to gain high positions for himself and his friends. Walter Stewart, after prolonged and menacing cross-examination, was ready to identify the elephant, the dromedary and indeed the whole menagerie with anyone they suggested to him. On this evidence and that of John Stewart, Montrose's enemies now had a formidable case against him.

The Committee of Estates ordered his arrest with that of Napier. But they did not order the release of John Stewart, who was beheaded a few weeks later. On the scaffold the poor man tried to explain that he had slandered Montrose, but it was too late by then to undo what he had done. With John Stewart dead and Walter Stewart intimidated,

Montrose now faced trial for treason and conspiracy with little to help him except his innocence. Still trusting in that, he clamoured for a public hearing so that he might justify himself and denounce his opponents.

His enemies were not so simple as to give him this opportunity. They drew up and made public a lengthy accusation, which Montrose described as a 'rhapsody of forethought villainy' on their part; they threatened a trial and talked darkly of chopping off heads. But they kept Montrose close in Edinburgh Castle and took good care that no public trial should take place.

Argyll needed to have Montrose out of the way chiefly because king Charles was at last coming to Scotland. He reached Edinburgh in August, when Montrose had been in prison for over a month, and he left in November. During that time the Scots Parliament met, under the domination of Argyll, and half forced, half persuaded the king to appoint a new council for Scotland entirely of their own choosing. They

Edinburgh Castle (Richard Foulsham)

compelled him also to make other concessions – to abandon the bishops and the Prayer Book finally, and to agree that the Covenant should be subscribed throughout the country.

Yet even from prison, the influence of Montrose gave Argyll some little trouble. He was still popular in spite of all that had been said against him – 'so gallant a gentleman and so well-beloved,' as one of the king's suite described him. A moderate centre party, which had almost come into being when the Cumbernauld Bond was signed, was still a possibility, and while it was a possibility it was a danger to Argyll. In order to end the danger once and for all he sought the alliance of Hamilton, the king's evil genius. Hamilton cared for little except his own greatness, and it was easy to persuade him that he had nothing to gain and everything to lose from the growth of a centre party in Scotland, which would threaten his ascendancy with the king. By such arguments Argyll persuaded Hamilton to enter into a highly elaborate plot. They were both to flee from Edinburgh as if in fear for their lives, and then declare that they had discovered a plot to seize Edinburgh castle, release Montrose, put him in charge of the army and kill the leaders of the Covenanters out of hand.

This ingenious invention is known to history as the *Incident* – an odd name for there was no *Incident* of any kind except the flight of Argyll and Hamilton. Even the mob did not altogether believe so very tall a story. But though no one quite believed it no one knew what to believe. This confusion was sufficient for Argyll's purpose. In the general atmosphere of suspicion, doubt and intimidation, king Charles felt his only safe course was to conciliate Argyll. His decision was accelerated by the news that an Irish rebellion of unparalleled violence and ferocity had broken out in Ulster. The king's presence was urgently required by his English Parliament. Before leaving Scotland he made Argyll a Marquess to ensure his loyalty and created Alexander Leslie Earl of Leven, apparently as a reward for defeating him. The king's neglected friends, in and out of prison, shrugged their shoulders and tried to laugh it off: next time, they said, they would rebel too, and no doubt they would be made earls and marquesses.

Argyll was now virtually the greatest man in Scotland. Sure of his position, he allowed Montrose and Napier to be released twenty-four hours before king Charles left Edinburgh. Their trial was postponed, then forgotten.

Argyll had got all that he wanted without it. He had destroyed Montrose's hope of forming a moderate party for the king; he had kept him from the royal presence; he had brought him within the shadow of the scaffold. He hoped and believed that, after his salutary shock the young gallant would leave politics to wiser heads and be the obedient tool of the Covenanting party.

He had misjudged his man. He had not heard the last of Montrose.

CHAPTER FOUR

HOPE DEFERRED

For the next year Montrose was at home at Kincardine. It was the last tranquil interlude during which he could be with his wife and children, watch his sons growing up, show them how to handle bow and rapier, read or talk with them, and wander, wet or fine, on horseback or on foot, over the hills of his home.

It was probably during this interlude that Montrose collected his ideas about politics, the fruit of his recent experience, in a letter to an unknown friend, probably Drummond of Hawthornden. Taking examples alike from contemporary Europe and ancient history, he argued that there could be no stable government without a strong central authority. Between the evil of absolutism on the one hand and of anarchy on the other, he saw a temperate monarchy as the ideal. But if there must be tyranny, he argued, that of the king, which cannot last for ever, is preferable to that of factions, 'where every man oppresseth his neighbour without any hope of redress from a prince despoiled of his power to punish oppressors'. It is not a very cheerful document; the once optimistic Montrose now gloomily contemplated the future as a choice of evils.

There was peace in Scotland. But in England king Charles and his Parliament had quarrelled beyond hope of reconciliation. On 22 August 1642 king Charles unfurled his standard at Nottingham. The Civil War had begun.

Both combatants looked anxiously towards Scotland. In accordance with king Charles's commands, the Scots had raised an army to quell the Irish rising. Some of this army went to Ireland, but by far the larger part remained in reserve in Scotland under the command of Lord Leven. In reserve for what emergency? This was a question to which

A true and exact Relation of the

manner of his Maiefties fetting up of His

Standard at *Nottingham*, on Munday the
22. of Auguſt 1642.

Firſt, The forme of the Standard, as it is here figured , and who were pre-
fent at the advancing of it

Secondly, The danger of fetting up of former Standards , and the damage
which enfued thereon.

Thirdly, A relation of all the Standards that ever were fet up by any King.

Fourthly, the names of thofe Knights who are appointed to be the Kings
Standard-bearers. With the forces that are appoynted to guard it.

Fifthly, The manner of the Kings comming firſt to *Coventry*.

Sixtly, The *Cavalieres* refolution and dangerous threats which they have
uttered, if the King concludes a peace without them. or hearkens unto
his great Councell the Parliament : Moreover how they have fhared
and divided *London* amongſt themfelves already.

Nottingham.

*A contemporary depiction of the raising of the Royal Standard at Nottingham on 22 August
1642 (Ashmolean Museum)*

the answer seemed obvious when the Scots appointed Commissioners to go to London to keep in touch with the English Parliament.

The king's very natural suspicions were however stifled because Hamilton, whom he sent to investigate, confidently assured him that Scotland would not enter the war. In Edinburgh, meanwhile, Hamilton had cemented his friendship with Argyll; it was rumoured that he was to marry one of Argyll's daughters. The king's friends in Scotland viewed these developments with the gravest distrust, and in March 1643 Montrose slipped across the Border to meet and warn Queen Henrietta Maria. The little French queen, who had been in the Low Countries raising money for her husband, received him well; she listened at first with intelligent sympathy to his warning that Argyll would come to an agreement with Parliament and send Leven's well-trained and powerful army against the king. Then Hamilton arrived at York, very splendid and majestic, with a suite of horsemen and attendants worthy of a prince. Arrogant and assured, he swept aside the reports of Montrose as no more than the fancies of a restless and disappointed intriguer.

Puzzled, the queen wrote to the king, at his headquarters in Oxford, and laid before him these conflicting accounts of Scotland. While she waited for an answer the two noblemen continued to frequent her Court in the pretty stone mansion known as the King's House at York. One day the tranquil court was disturbed by the furious snarling and growling of a dogfight. Hamilton, perceiving that the queen's frightened ladies expected something of him, flashed out his sword and ran it through the nearest dog. The poor beast dropped dead on the instant. No one was much impressed by this violent way of dealing with the dogs, and Montrose, who had all a sportsman's dislike of the business, composed a rhymed epigram which was not flattering to Hamilton. It was not meant for his eyes, but no doubt some malicious person showed it to him.

Henrietta Maria, after Van Dyck, c. 1632–5 (National Portrait Gallery)

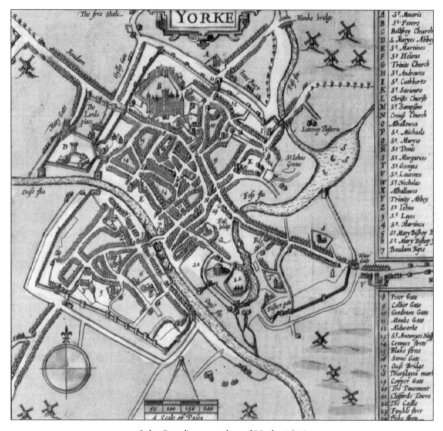

John Speed's town plan of York, 1610

> *Here lies a dog whose qualities did plead*
> *Such fatal end from a renowned blade,*
> *And blame him not though he succumbéd now,*
> *For Hercules could not combat 'gainst two;*
> *For whilst he on his foe revenge did take*
> *He manfully was killed behind his back.*
> *Then say, to eternise the cur that's gone:*
> *He fleshed the maiden sword of Hamilton.*

Hamilton, who was sensitive about his military prowess, was deeply offended. But he had his revenge. Within a few days the awaited letter came from king Charles. He accepted Hamilton's report of Scots affairs. There was nothing for Montrose to do but return home disconsolate.

It was for Argyll and his party to rejoice. They believed Montrose to be ambitious; they knew him to be a soldier of unusual gifts. Now that the king had rejected him, they assumed that he was ripe for their own designs.

Montrose had not long returned from York when a visitor came to Kincardine. This was Sir James Rollo who many years before had married his sister Dorothy. Dorothy had died young and Rollo had taken as his second wife a sister of Argyll. He was thus in the odd position of being brother-in-law to both of them. Rollo had been sent to tell Montrose that his old friends of the Covenant could still find an important command for him in their army if he were willing.

Montrose said neither yes nor no, but asked for a more definite statement. In response to this the Committee of Estates sent Alexander Henderson to talk to him. They met not far from Stirling on the banks of Allan water and talked a long time in the open air. They were two men who respected each other's opinions, whatever shifting of political parties had brought them into opposition. There seems to be very little doubt that Henderson made it clear that the Covenanters wanted Montrose to lead their army himself if it came to an alliance with Parliament and an invasion of England. We cannot know what success he hoped for in putting forward this proposition for he did not, like Argyll, think of Montrose as an ambitious man set on his own aggrandizement. He probably hoped that Montrose's resolute religious convictions would turn the scale with him as between king and Covenant, should it come to war again.

Montrose was indeed unshaken in his religious beliefs, but he had seen the Kirk too shamelessly used for political ends in Scotland for him to trust in the sincerity of the governing party on that score. For him the question posed itself in political terms only: how best to preserve the authority of the Crown against the self-interest of the dominant faction.

He could not accept Henderson's offer. But, with a soldier's sense of the situation, he recognized the extreme peril in which he stood should he refuse it once it had been made. He asked Henderson whether he had full authority to negotiate with him and when Henderson hesitated, he put him off for the time being unanswered.

Immediately afterwards he left Scotland, vanishing from his home and friends almost without farewells and taking with him his cousin Lord Ogilvie. With all speed the two made their way to join the king in England, sure that this time Charles must believe the truth about the imminent danger from Scotland.

But Charles, a man of fixed opinions, would not listen. All that autumn Montrose and Ogilvie stayed in Oxford, seeking in vain to convince the king and his councillors of Argyll's intentions. In the general hubbub round the king their voices were hardly heeded. Oxford was alive with intrigue. The once quiet university town was now noisy with troops and lively with the feverish gaiety of a city at war. The wives and daughters of the king's troops crammed every

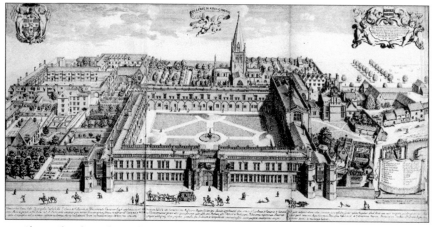

Christ Church, Oxford, where the king lived while in residence in the city (The Bodleian Library, Oxford, Arch.A.11.13. Plate 27.)

51

house and the queen's ladies fluttered in silks through precincts once sacred to learning. Prince Rupert's cavalry drilled in the wide meadows beyond Christ Church; parties of horse clattered out at nightfall to harry the rebel garrisons in the Chiltern hills, and clattered back at first light flushed with ephemeral triumph. It was possible for an active young man to volunteer for such raiding parties, and Montrose may well, from time to time, have served as a private soldier under one of Rupert's captains on some night venture in the hills.

But in the main it was a time of frustration and anxiety, of vain waiting in ante-rooms and useless interviews with those who would not or could not listen to his warning. He had personal anxieties besides this greater one for the king's cause. We cannot know what passed between him and his wife Magdalen before he left his home, but she had never cared for his wild ideas and her cautious family strongly disapproved of any action which might endanger her and her children. She may have felt like Shakespeare's Lady Macduff:

> *Wisdom! to leave his wife, to leave his babes,*
> *His mansion and his titles in a place*
> *From whence himself does fly! He loves us not. . . .*

She did not want to see Kincardine burnt before her eyes as poor Lady Ogilvie had seen the Bonnie House of Airlie. In her difficulty she withdrew more and more from her husband's friends into the secure shelter of her own cautiously time-serving family.

This was perhaps the background of the famous love song which Montrose seems to have written at about this date. He was only following the literary fashion of the time when he took his similes from current politics, yet he may have had his wife's political estrangement in mind when he accused her, in these pretty and gallant verses, of holding a synod in her heart, as the meetings of Calvinist divines were called.

My dear and only Love, I pray,
That little world of thee
Be governed by no other sway
Than purest monarchy.
For if confusion have a part,
Which virtuous souls abhor,
And hold a Synod in thine heart,
I'll never love thee more.

Like Alexander I will reign,
And I will reign alone;
My thoughts did ever more disdain
A rival on my throne.
He either fears his fate too much,
Or his deserts are small,
That dares not put it to the touch,
To gain or lose it all.

And in the Empire of thine heart,
Where I should solely be,
If others do pretend a part
Or dare to vie with me,
Or Committees if thou erect
And go on such a score,
I'll laugh and sing at thy neglect,
And never love thee more.

But if thou wilt prove faithful then,
And constant of thy word,
I'll make thee glorious by my pen
And famous by my sword.

I'll serve thee in such noble ways
Was never heard before;
I'll crown and deck thee all with bays
And love thee more and more.

Meanwhile, in October the Scots signed an alliance with Parliament on whom they forced, in return for their alliance, a new and yet more stringent Covenant, called the Solemn League and Covenant. Charles did not fully believe the news until he heard in mid-December that Lord Leven had fixed the rendezvous for his army at Berwick on New Year's Day. Then, too late, light broke on him. He had just, rather inconveniently, made Hamilton a duke. This could not be undone, but the new duke was not well received when he next came to Oxford. What had he now to say, the king indignantly asked, to explain his repeated assurance that the Scots would remain neutral in the war?

Hamilton was no whit abashed. He had undertaken, he said, that the Scots should remain neutral for the whole of that year. If His Majesty would pause to consider the dates, he would perceive that the projected date for Lord Leven's invasion was *New Year's Day*. He had therefore kept his promise. Such affrontery was too much even for Charles. Hamilton, to his great surprise, found himself under arrest. Montrose's moment had come.

Two allies now appeared to help him, Lord Aboyne and Lord Antrim. Aboyne, the active second son of Huntly against whom Montrose had fought at Brig o' Dee, had been in attendance on the king since the beginning of the war. Disappointed because his own father took no action for the king in Scotland, he now transferred his enthusiasm to Montrose.

Antrim, the handsome, brainless chief of the Irish Macdonalds, had never yet been able to make good against Argyll that grant of Kintyre given him by the king five years before. He now offered to send over ten thousand of his clan from Ireland to land in Galloway. If Montrose

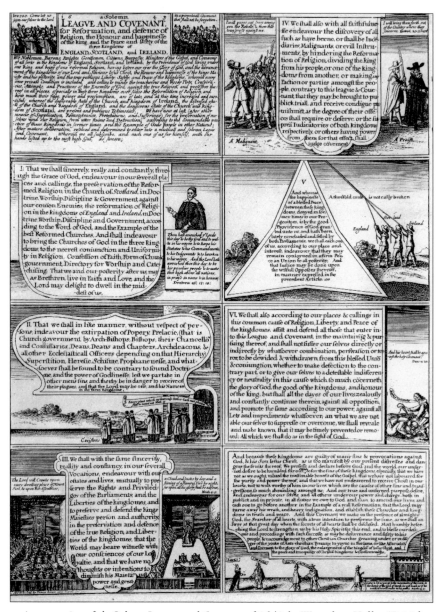

An engraving of the Solemn League and Covenant of 1643 by Wenceslaus Hollar (British Museum)

could cross the Border with a part of the English army and join these Irish there would be force sufficient to frighten Argyll into recalling Lord Leven's army from England.

Montrose did not think highly of Antrim, but he knew the value of the Macdonalds as fighters. Rapidly the plan of action took shape. Antrim would cross to Ireland to get his people ready. Montrose and Aboyne would go to the king's northern headquarters at York with permission to take command of as large a force of horse and foot as could be spared. They would then invade Scotland, and wait in Galloway until the Macdonalds joined them.

It looked hopeful on paper. Charles signed Montrose's commission as Lieutenant-Governor and Captain General in Scotland in February 1644. Before the end of the month he presented himself at York. Here came the first serious hitch. The Scots army had crossed the Border into England five weeks before and every Royalist soldier in the north was needed to hold them in check. A hundred horse was all that could be spared for Montrose. He could not invade Scotland with a hundred horse. But he got permission to recruit as best he could in the north-west, and after four weeks preparation in Cumberland he crossed the Border at Gretna Green with nearly two thousand horse and foot, an achievement which showed what could be done by a man who could organize as well as lead.

On the occasion of this return to Scotland he drafted a manifesto which is interesting because it shows with what tenacity he stood by the principles which he had once believed to be embodied in the Covenant. He had come, he said, to defend 'the true Protestant religion, His Majesty's just and sacred authority, the fundamental laws and privileges of Parliaments, the peace and freedom of the oppressed and thralled subject'. Next, with that extraordinary candour which characterized so much of what he said and did, he asserted that he would not himself have taken arms for the king were he not convinced of the king's intention to defend the religion and rights of his people.

'Did I but see the least appearance of His Majesty's change from these resolutions,' he wrote, he would not himself 'longer continue my faithful endeavours.'

This manifesto does not appear to have been printed and it is very improbable that king Charles ever saw it, which was just as well as it would have shocked him profoundly. In his opinion a subject owed his 'faithful endeavours' to the king as an unquestioning duty, not as something conditional on his own good behaviour.

The invasion of Galloway took Argyll completely by surprise. Before he realized what had happened the town of Dumfries had thrown open its gates to Montrose. On hearing the news in Oxford, king Charles decided to reward his new champion with the title of Marquess, but while the documents were being drawn up, Montrose had met with a check. Argyll, with all the forces he could raise, was fast advancing on the small band at Dumfries and there was still no sign of the promised ten thousand Macdonalds.

Loth to go back, but unable to hold Dumfries against superior forces, Montrose tried to slip across the lowland moors to the country north of Stirling which he believed he could raise for the king. But his English troops refused to go so far from home. They mutinied and he had to retire as best he could to Carlisle, there to wait for definite news of Antrim.

While waiting, he was not idle. From his headquarters at Carlisle he scoured the country against the Scots, going so far afield as to relieve the pressure on Newcastle by driving them out of Morpeth. With continual recruiting he succeeded in raising a substantial force of Westmorland and Cumberland men to hold their county for the king against the Covenanting Scots. But there was still no news from Antrim, and the summer was fast going by.

Unparalleled and unexpected disaster now followed. York, hard pressed by the Scots under Leven and the Parliamentarians under Fairfax, sent an appeal for help to the king. Prince Rupert, with the flower of his cavalry, made a spectacular march to the rescue, but on

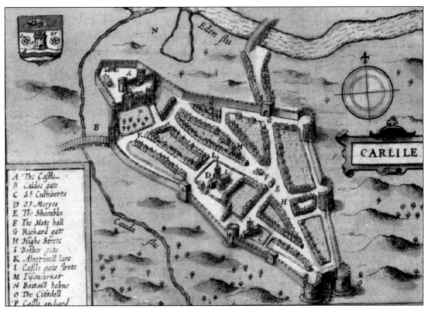

A The Castle
B Caldoe gate
C St Cuthberts
D St Maryes
E The Shambles
F The Mote hall
G Richard gate
H Highe Streete
I Bother gate
K Abbeywell lane
L Castle gate streete
M Fishmarket
N Battaill holme
O The Citadell
P Castle orchard

John Speed's town plan of Carlisle, 1610

2 July 1644 he was fatally and totally defeated at Marston Moor. Montrose, who had been hurrying to his help, came up with Rupert's dispirited and broken remnant at Richmond in Yorkshire. For several days his fresh and efficient cavalry guarded the Royalist retreat. In the evenings he discussed plans with Rupert. The situation in England was very grave; something had to be done to strengthen the Royalist army. Rupert had little choice but to take over Montrose's forces to heal the gashes in his own.

Montrose made no difficulties. He was too good a soldier not to see that the prince's immediate need must be served. Besides, he still had no news of Antrim. Alone but for his original hundred horse, Aboyne, Ogilvie, and a few other officers, he made his way to the last Royalist outpost in the north-east, Newcastle. No one there could give him any help, and he turned back to his old headquarters at Carlisle. His whole scheme for raising Scotland had fallen to the ground.

Prince Rupert by Gerard Honthorst (National Portrait Gallery, London)

This was the moment at which a man of less intense determination than Montrose would have given up. But he would not admit defeat. It had been impossible safely to reach his friends north of Stirling with a small army; but supposing he should go alone? The plan was no sooner thought of than put into execution. He chose only two companions, an old professional soldier, Colonel Sibbald, and William Rollo, the younger brother of Sir James Rollo, who was one of his closest friends. Rollo had been lame from birth and could not walk well, but he could do anything on a horse. Taking what money they had, the king's commission and the Royal Standard concealed in the lining of a saddle, the three of them would set out innocently to Scotland – two gentlemen travelling on their private affairs, and a groom, leading an extra horse. Aboyne was to wait in the north for news. Ogilvie was to go back to Oxford and report to the king.

One August morning, therefore, two soldierly-looking gentlemen, one young and the other grizzled, rode northwards from Carlisle across the fells, followed at a respectful distance by a groom, leading a better horse than the one he rode. The groom was the best horseman of the three.

CHAPTER FIVE

THE CHASE BEGINS

There were not many people on the roads and those they passed paid no great attention to them. But one man turned and stared at the groom. 'Good day, my Lord,' he said. 'You are mistaken,' the groom protested, but the other shook his head with a sly enigmatic smile. 'What, do I not know my Lord of Montrose well enough?' he said. 'But go on your way and God be with you.'

Who he was they never found out, but at any rate he kept their secret. In four days they reached Montrose's first objective, the house of Tulliebelton on the verge of the Highlands. Here lived one of his greatest friends and his close kinsman, Patrick Graham of Inchbrakie, called 'Black Pate' on account of a dark disfigurement to his face caused long since by an explosion of gunpowder.

Montrose lay concealed in the heather above Tulliebelton where Inchbrakie brought him food and news. There was a rumour that the Irish Macdonalds had landed, a rumour which was confirmed within a few days when a tall Highlander strode into the house of Tulliebelton and asked Black Pate if he knew where he could deliver a letter for Montrose.

Black Pate kept his own counsel but took the letter. On the hillside among the heather Montrose broke the seal; it was from Alasdair Macdonald, the youthful warrior to whom Antrim had entrusted the leadership of his forces. They had landed in Kintyre, and had struck north-eastwards into the Highlands intending to join with other Macdonalds in those parts, and were now cut off in Badenoch, with the Campbell country behind them and they knew not what in front. Montrose sent immediate orders that they were to march to Blair Atholl and there expect him.

After years of disappointment and months of delay, events now moved with dizzy speed. As the Macdonalds marched, the clans in Atholl took up arms and came together *against* them. In the Highlands the politics of Edinburgh, Oxford and London were very far away. The threatened clans did not pause to ask the Macdonalds if they were friends or foes; it was enough that they were coming with swords in their hands. By the time Alasdair reached the Braes of Atholl, the Stewarts and the Robertsons were under arms to meet him. They faced each other where the silent river Tilt flows down from the huge bare mountains of Atholl to join the brawling Garry, and the country opens out for a few miles into a soft valley of green pastures. Camped on the heathery slopes above, the armed clans watched each other stealthily in the eye of the August sun.

Glen Tilt near Blair Atholl end, an ancient route from the central Lowlands into the eastern Highlands (Jim Henderson)

Before they could join battle there appeared between them, walking swiftly over the hills, two gentlemen in Highland dress. The one with the swarthy, black disfigurement of face was well known in all that region as Black Pate of Inchbrakie, but it was a few moments before they recognized his companion. Then it went from lip to lip along the ranks of the gathered clans. The Macdonalds threw up their caps and fired a salvo with their remaining powder. Montrose had come.

The hardest task yet remained, for Montrose had come to lead the Macdonalds, and the clans of Atholl had come to fight them. He called their leaders out between the ranks, showed them the king's commission and explained the need to unite against his enemies. The clan from Ireland were not invaders but allies, not strangers and enemies but Gaels from the Western Highlands come to avenge a wrong against the Campbells and to join with them in fighting the enemies of the king. Before the sun went down behind the western hills he had the leaders of all parties gathered together in friendship. Alasdair Macdonald towered above them all, the splendid seven-foot giant who led the Irish clan. His father, poetically named Colkitto – or he who fights with both hands – had been driven from Kintyre by Argyll and he himself, born in exile in Ireland, had grown to manhood among old tales and bardic prophecies which made him the hero and avenger of his people. His father even now lay a prisoner in one of Arygll's dungeons awaiting the liberating sword of his son.

Two days later, on 28 August, Montrose raised the Royal Standard. With a triumphant fanfare of trumpets and the fierce skirling of the pipes, the crushed silken folds, so long compressed in the lining of his saddle, fluttered free on the northern breeze – their king's standard, sent by their king's command from far in the south, and carried to them by the hand of his own General.

Montrose himself had assumed the Highland dress, with a bunch of yellow oats for a badge stuck in his bonnet, and a broadsword in his hand. He had by nature much sympathy with the Highland character – the swift, powerful enthusiasm, the lyric inspiration in danger, the quick impulsive heart and hand. There was, now and to the end of his life, a natural understanding between him and the men he led.

But he had also a good deal of the cautious, stubborn character of the Lowland Grahams. If he felt, standing by the king's standard, in the centre of his Highland host, an exhilaration such as he had never felt before, he could see well enough, when he sat with his officers round the council table that evening, that he had singularly little cause for confidence.

Antrim had promised to send ten thousand men. Montrose had probably not counted on the full ten thousand, but it may have been a shock to learn that the full number of the Irish was hardly eleven hundred. Furthermore, they had almost exhausted their ammunition long before they reached the braes of Atholl. The Stewarts and Robertsons swelled Montrose's army to something over two thousand men, but they were untrained and armed only with dirks and swords. Apart from the ponies which carried the baggage, there were exactly three horses in the army.

There was another problem. Highland enthusiasm is vehement but not lasting. Montrose must act at once, or the army would grow bored and mutinous and drift away home. On the following day he marched, following the course of the Garry eastwards, then striking south over the moors to Aberfeldy and so down Glen Almond to the vale of Perth. By the way he met three hundred men under a kinsman of his own who had taken up arms against a possible attack from the wild Macdonalds. He showed them the king's commission and they, too, like the Stewarts and the Robertsons, joined his army.

Four miles west of Perth, round the little village of Tippermuir, extends a wide uneven tableland, falling away steeply at its eastern edge towards the sheltered city.

This was the ground chosen by the Covenanting defenders of Perth,

to stop Montrose. There were about six
thousand of them, well armed and well
provided. But they were mostly local
troops, hurriedly raised, with a stiffening of
two regiments from the south. Their
principal advantages were: strong
contingents of cavalry to cover their flanks,
guns and ammunition and more than twice
Montrose's numbers.

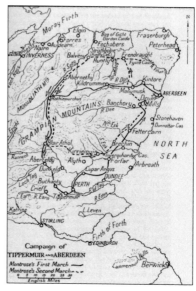

*Plan of the Campaign of Tippermuir and
Perth*

Montrose's advantages were the violent
courage and speed of his men. How could
he make these qualities tell against his
opponents, stolidly deployed in front of him
in formal battle order, with cavalry and
muskets?

Shock was the answer. He gave them no
time. His musketeers fired a volley with
the last of the ammunition. Then, under cover of the smoke, the
Highlanders charged. The astonished lowlanders were still
wondering what had hit them, when the force of the Highland
charge had smashed clean through their front line. The rout was
total.

It was not of course as easy as that sounds. But that was the
principle of it. Before nightfall on that eventful first of September
Montrose and his Highlanders entered Perth in triumph.

He stayed in Perth for three days, time enough for his two elder
boys to ride over from Kincardine to see him. John, Lord Graham, was
now fourteen, James nearly twelve, both young for the kind of
campaigning that their father foresaw ahead of him in the next
months. But his enemies might use his sons as hostages if he left them
unprotected at home. James, he decided, was too young for them to
touch, but John, his heir, and therefore the more important of the two,

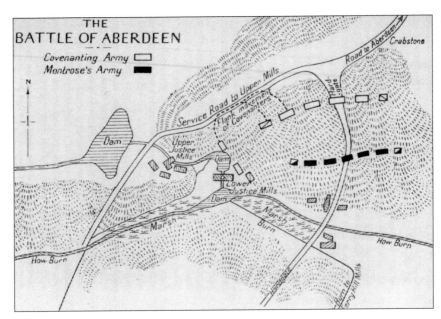

Plan of the Battle of Aberdeen

would be in real danger. Whatever the perils of the coming campaign, John had better stay with him.

Montrose now had to face and solve certain military problems. He could not, like Rupert or Cromwell, gather and keep in being a body of men and train them to fight together. Wherever he went in the Highlands he would be able to raise here a hundred men and there fifty and here two hundred, who would follow him *under their own chieftain* for a month, or several months, or maybe only for a fortnight, and then go home again, to rejoin him later if it suited them. He could not discipline these shifting forces in any usual fashion, for they would only obey their own chiefs, and if their chiefs fell out among themselves, chaotic disorder might ensue. It very nearly did when Stewart of Ardvorlich stabbed Lord Kinpont in a private quarrel two days after Tippermuir, but Stewart fled and Montrose managed to calm the rising disorder.

There was one other problem – that of religion. The Irish Macdonalds were Catholic; so were some of the other Highland clans – but not all. Montrose himself was a Calvinist as were most of his Graham supporters, the Robertsons and many of the Stewarts. Yet such was his tact and management that no religious trouble ever divided his army. This peculiar rabble of men could give an example to all Europe, for both religions were practised, in amity, side by side.

Montrose's enemies declared that he either could not or would not control his wild forces. There was certainly a good deal of plundering and burning during his campaigns but this was an inevitable accompaniment of the desperate war that he was now waging; it was no more serious than that inflicted by his opponents. He set his face resolutely against unnecessary slaughter or the ill-treatment of prisoners and, on almost all occasions, managed to enforce his will in this respect. Contemporary evidence, where it is untouched by propaganda, suggests that his discipline was, by the standards of the time, exceptionally good. The secret of his control over his varied and capricious following, lay in his personality. As a contemporary Highland writer puts it, his courtesy, simplicity and charm 'quickly made a conquest of the hearts of all his followers, so as when he list he could have led them in a chain to have followed him with cheerfulness in all his enterprises'.

Montrose had to overcome the professional troops of the Covenant with a fluctuating band of untrained men, whom he held together by vigilant diplomacy and commanded by persuasion, argument and a kind of flowery rhetoric, for they would have been offended by terse military orders. His tactics would have to be those of speed and shock while his strategy depended on the difficult geography of the Highland mountains. He planned, therefore, to deliver a series of sudden, sharp attacks on the chief garrisons of the enemy within striking distance of the Highlands. Then he would fall back, drawing the Lowland armies after him. Once in the defiles of the

Loveing freindes

Being heir, for the maintenaning of Religion and liberty and his Maiesties just authority and servility thes ar, in his Maiesties name to requyre yow that immediatly upon the sight heirof yow rander and give up your toune in the behalf of his Maiestie Otherwayes that all old persons women and children doe come out and reteire themselfs, and that those who stayes expect no quarter I am

(Indorse)

Loveing freindes
 Being heir, for the maintenaning of Religion and liberty and his Maiesties just authority and servility thes ar, in his Maiesties name to requyre yow that immediatly upon the sight heirof yow rander and give up your toune in the behalf of his Maiestie Otherwayes that all old persons women and children doe come out and reteire themselfs, and that those who stayes expect no quarter I am

> As you deserve
> MONTROSE.

Montrose's letter to the Town Council of Aberdeen demanding the surrender of the town
(Aberdeen Town Council)

~~Most~~ noble Lord

gentilman and a

We have receavit yors with a ∧ Drumer qrby yor/ Lo/ signifies to ws yt you ar for mantinaince of Religione Liberty and his maties just authoritie and yt we suld rander our toune, wtherwayes no

our selfis

quarter is except to old persones weemen and children, We acknawledge Lykwayes oblige to manteine the same quhilkis yor lo/ professes ~~to ws~~ you ar doing and sall be most willing to spend the Last Drope

according to the

of our blood yrin, ~~without prejudice of the first and Latter~~ covenant ~~is~~ subt and sworn by us   Yor/ Lo/

will   abandoune   yt we deserve

must have us excused yt we ~~can~~ not ∧ render our toune so Lichtly, seing we think ~~our selfis not worthy~~

no

~~of a~~ censure as being guiltie of the breatche of any the affoirsaidis poyntis and speciallie of yt latter articles bot have beine evir knawin to be most Loyall and dewtiefull subjectis to His matie and by gods grace sall to our Lyves end stryve to continow, so, and in the meane tyme to be

as ye deserve

Yor/ Lo/ ~~faithfull servands~~

~~to serve you~~

Provost and baillies of abd
in name of the burghe

abd yis 13 7ber 1644
at allevin acloak

The reply sent by the Provost and Baillies of Aberdeen to Montrose's letter on the previous page.
The battle began immediately after Montrose's receipt of the letter (Aberdeen Town Council)

mountains he could turn and fight on ground which his troops understood.

On leaving Perth Montrose marched first towards Dundee but the town was too strongly held and he headed northwards for Aberdeen. Here a Covenanting garrison of three thousand men was in occupation. Montrose's summons was rejected. He was still at this time uncertain of the temper of his troops and he thought it wise to warn the authorities in Aberdeen to send their women and children and infirm to a place of safety in the event of attack; the warning, which proved to be only too well founded, went unheeded. The messenger whom Montrose had sent to the city was accompanied by a drummer boy; as the two retraced their steps to the camp the child was shot, deliberately, by one of the Covenanting musketeers. The outrage seems to have been the final exasperation to Montrose's excitable troops.

The garrison, trusting to their numbers, drew out before the town intending to outflank and annihilate Montrose's small force. Again, as at Tippermuir, but this time with more ammunition and a handful of skirmishing cavalry on his wings, he concentrated on shattering the centre of their line before they could surround him. Once again the impact of the Irish charge broke the enemy centre but here there was not, as at Perth, the saving four miles of pursuit, so that the Irish fury was spent before the town was reached. Here pursuers and pursued entered the city gates immediately together and citizens fell with soldiers in desperate disordered street fighting and the plunder which ensued.

But now Argyll, in person, at the head of four thousand men, horse and foot, the best that the south could provide, was hurrying to the rescue. Montrose waited until he was within two days' march and then started northwards as if to the Gordon country. When he was sure that Argyll and his army were labouring after him, he struck suddenly west, reached Speyside and hurried up the valley of the Spey at the pace that only Highland troops could go.

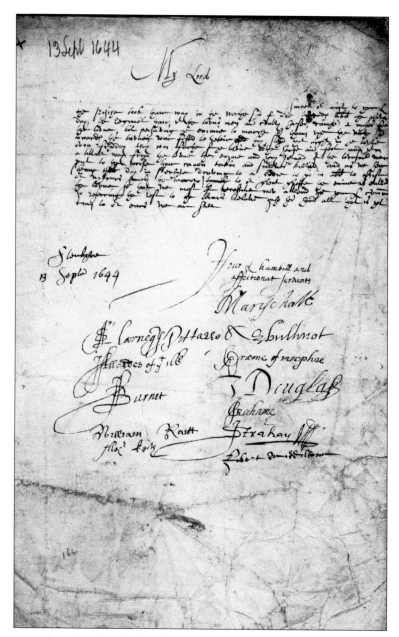

Letter from Lord Marischal and others to the Earl of Argyll, 13 September 1644,
informing him of Montrose's victory at Aberdeen and his entry into the town
(Scottish Record Office PA7/23/2/25)

Argyll lumbered north in his tracks, lost the scent, picked it up again, wheeled south-west and struggled after him up the Spey, traversing for four interminable, slow and anxious days the forest of Rothiemurchus. The autumn weather was sultry and overcast; all the trees looked alike, and every rocky cleft might be an ambush. Argyll's men had no certain news of Montrose. He had passed that way – one day before, five days before – accounts differed. He might have hidden in any of the narrow glens running down to Speyside from the purple massif of Cairngorm. While they traversed Rothiemurchus, hungry, tired, and baffled, Montrose was already laughing at them from the huge bare uplands of Badenoch. By the time they emerged he was back where he had started from, in the braes of Atholl.

Stubborn and raging, Argyll compelled his unwilling troops to drag on, in their buff coats and heavy boots over the pathless moors, by bog and scree, where the light Highlanders moved as easily as deer.

Argyll may have expected Montrose to wait for him at Blair Atholl. That was, after all, where he had unfurled the king's standard and where presumably he had his base. But Montrose's mobile forces hardly needed a base. They carried all they had with them. They had no guns, no stores; if need be they could keep moving for months at a time, sleeping on the heather, wet or fine, drinking stream water and eating the flesh of the game they killed or a little uncooked oatmeal. Their plaids served them for cloaks, blankets and bedding; sometimes even for stranger purposes. A priest, who marched with them, tells how in the driving wet and rain two or three tall Highlanders would make a curtain with their plaids about an improvised altar to guard the flickering candles from the wind as he celebrated Mass.

As Argyll's men dragged themselves over the desolate waste of Badenoch, Montrose marched merrily out of Blair, down the Garry, Tummel and Tay to Dunkeld. Hence he struck eastward towards the coast, passed through Brechin – startling his wife's relations at Kinnaird – and entered his own Montrose, where the people came crowding out to welcome him and entertained his troops on the best that their cellars and larders could afford. After a week's rest in this delightful haven he had news that Argyll and his men were just emerging from the hills of Angus on to the Brechin road. Within a few hours, in the highest of spirits, Montrose headed north again. It was now the third week of October; the days were growing shorter and colder. Argyll would not be able to keep his sulky southern troops on the march for many weeks more. If Montrose intended to give them a last encounter to remember him by, before the winter, he would have to stop the wild-goose chase and stand to fight.

He occupied Fyvie Castle, whence, if the encounter with Argyll proved unsuccessful, he could fall back swiftly and easily into the

Rehearsals for the July 1994 re-enactment of the Battle of Fyvie by the Sealed Knot Society in front of Fyvie Castle (Jim Henderson)

mountains. Argyll was unlikely to follow. His men had trailed after Montrose for the best part of two hundred and fifty miles in a complete circle through the hardest country in Scotland; he would never get them to start on that round again.

It took the labouring southerners five days to come up with their quarry. Montrose meanwhile had thrown up earthworks in front of Fyvie Castle. His chief problem was ammunition, for his men had used all that they had captured at Tippermuir and Aberdeen. He martialled the domestic plate of Fyvie – candlesticks, canisters, thimbles and all, even the metal bands round the wine-casks – and had them melted for bullets. Powder was a more serious problem for they had little left. In the first day's fighting they made the deficiency good by capturing some of Argyll's, and after forty-eight hours of hot skirmishing among the trenches and copses about Fyvie, Argyll fell back with heavy losses. Montrose slipped away into the mountains and left him, deluded, sore and raging.

Montrose now called his staff into council. During his marches he had been joined not only by troops of Highlanders but by many lairds and gentlemen from Perthshire or even farther south. The dance they had led Argyll had been entertaining enough, for the weather had been reasonably good, and they had not had much more risk or anxiety than on a hunting expedition. Even so, some of these southern allies had found the going hard. But what they had done was nothing to what they might now have to do. The cold and violent northern winter lay before them, and Montrose had no intention of going to ground among the glens and waiting for the spring.

The Highlanders could keep on the march through the mountains in sleet and frost, wind and snow; so could the other clans of whose help Montrose had hopes. But could the Perthshire gentry? Most of them thought they could not, though the stout-hearted Lord Airlie and his sons were exceptions. The rest of them took farewell of him until the spring.

With reduced forces Montrose retraced his steps to Blair Atholl. It was mid-November when an early snowfall caught his troops struggling through the Grampian passes. The cold was bitter by day and worse by night; the frozen winds whistled down from the peaks, their plaids were hard with ice, they could find no dry firewood under the snow and little game to fill their hungry mouths. But they staggered at last into the sheltered hollow of Blair Atholl, thawed their clothes, filled their bellies, and, within twenty-four hours, were ready for anything.

CHAPTER SIX

A FAR CRY TO LOCH AWE

The Irish Macdonalds had long hoped that their clansmen of Scotland would join them. At Blair, in early December, two of their chiefs came in with a varied following; they were Macdonald of Glengarry and Macdonald of Clanranald.

Montrose had now occupied the castle of Blair, and here, in the glowing warmth of peat fires, he sat in council with the Macdonald chiefs. They were all alike of one mind. Elated by the success of the autumn, they wanted – as they thought – to end the war at a blow by breaking the Campbell clan in their own country.

The Campbells were fortunate in many ways, not least in having the chief seat of their clan in the most inaccessible corner of the south-western Highlands on the spit of land between Loch Fyne and Loch Linnhe. In the heart of this mountainous region stretches the long inland expanse of Loch Awe. Hence the mocking Campbell saying: 'It is a far cry to Loch Awe.' They believed that no enemy could penetrate to their land. This was exactly what the Macdonald chiefs, and above all Alasdair, had now set their hearts on doing. They would march at dead of winter when no one was stirring and smite the Campbells at Loch Awe; they would smite Argyll himself in his impregnable stronghold of Inveraray at the head of Loch Fyne.

Montrose took advantage of a mild spell in mid-December, crossed from Blair into the Tay valley, followed it up to Killin, where the final council of war was held, and the dangerous decision to invade the Campbell country was confirmed. Three days' march brought them to the head of Loch Awe where they sacked a village of the M'Corquodales, a sept under Campbell protection. Neither the people nor their chief stayed to fight, and Argyll, sitting down to dinner in

Kilchurn Castle on Loch Awe (The Royal Commission on the Ancient and Historical
Monuments of Scotland)

his castle at Inveraray twelve miles off, was called in amazement from his board to find the M'Corquodales and a score of his clansmen, wild with flight and fear, babbling incoherently of Montrose and the Macdonalds.

Argyll did not believe that an army even of Highlanders could attack Inveraray from the landward side, so well was it protected by ridge upon ridge of mountains. He thought the fugitives were exaggerating, to cover their own cowardice. Montrose on Loch Awe at the head of his forces? Nonsense. A hundred roving Macdonalds at most.

Not until the invaders were half-way down the glen and his own scouts reported the fatal truth did he believe it, and then it was too late to think of defence. He hurried to the shore with his family, boarded

Plan of the Campaign of Inverlochy

the ship that he always kept in readiness, and left his clansmen to the mercy of Montrose.

It was a bad winter for the Campbells. 'We left neither house nor hold unburned, nor corn, nor cattle, that belonged to the whole name of Campbell,' proudly reported one of Alasdair Macdonald's men. There was, however, little blodshed. Montrose had given reiterated orders against it, which he found all the easier to enforce as the Campbells had mostly followed their chief's example, and fled from their houses and villages to the cold comfort of the mountains.

In Edinburgh there was anger and dismay. General Baillie, an experienced veteran, was appointed to go against Montrose, while Argyll sent to Ireland to recall the best of his own soldiers, Duncan Campbell of Auchinbreck, and the two well-trained Campbell regiments he had with him.

With these substantial forces about to move against him, Montrose saw that he must get his men out of the Campbell country before they were trapped. He could not go back the way he had come for Baillie could easily block the Tay valley. He decided, therefore, to do the unexpected, to make for the inaccessible wilds of Lochaber, keeping well to the west. Two long inlets cut across his route to Lochaber; he would have to get his straggling forces, heavy with booty, first across Loch Etive and then across Loch Leven, in midwinter, with every possibility of storm and snow.

They began the march immediately after Christmas and crossed Loch Etive, near Dunstaffnage Castle, where they managed to find and

Glencoe in winter (David Paterson)

repair one large boat to carry forty men and three small ones to carry five apiece. For two days and two nights, in bright cold sunlight and bright moonlight, the one large boat and the three small ones crossed and re-crossed the narrow water until the whole host was on the farther side.

Argyll, with a newly gathered force of Campbells, was following on the rear and his armed ships patrolled the sea. Montrose zig-zagged and found his way to Loch Leven by way of the desolate pass of Glencoe. At nightfall he stood in drenching rain by the iron waters of the loch and could see not a boat in sight. Straight across the narrow water lowered the dark mountains where he could count on comparative safety. But how to get his men across? It was his worst moment, for he could not conceive why Argyll, who had shipping, did not land a force, however small, at the egress to Glencoe and so cut off his escape.

Argyll did nothing because he had made a plan with Baillie and, fortunately for Montrose, he stuck to the letter of the plan instead of seizing his opportunities as they arose. When it became clear that Montrose was making for Lochaber, his enemies saw a chance of trapping him. He could not stay in Lochaber for ever because there was too little to eat; he would have to come out, most probably into the Great Glen which cleaves like a deep gash diagonally across the heart of the Highlands. Argyll was to watch Montrose's rear and as soon as he came down into the Glen he was to seal its southern end at Inverlochy – near to the modern town of Fort William. At the same time Baillie was to stop up all possibility of his escaping through the mountains on the eastward side, and Seaforth, the chief of the Mackenzies, at this time much under Argyll's influence, was to march down the Great Glen from Inverness and take Montrose in front. When he was thoroughly embroiled Argyll was to fall on his rear. Argyll, therefore, thinking only of the trap prepared for Montrose in the Great Glen, made no attempt to fall on him at an earlier time.

On the following morning Montrose found some boats that his scouts had missed in the dusk, and the long crossing began. It was achieved without interruption, but the respite was only temporary. They could not stay for ever in that desolate country of barren and gigantic hills among which were only a few sparse settlements. The weather had, moreover, deteriorated. The rains were followed by two days of heavy snow which blotted out the mountains and choked the passes. Montrose had halted at the grey fortress of Inverlochy at the head of Loch Linnhe with the gigantic bastion of Ben Nevis towering above. It was a Campbell outpost but had not yet been manned. Leaving it behind him, he turned cautiously north-westward up the cleft of the Great Glen, following the river Lochy, with the wilds of Lochaber on his right. Here to the north he had the friendly Camerons and to the south the Macdonalds of Keppoch. But Seaforth, with all his forces, was fast marching down the glen to meet him, while in his rear Argyll and Auchinbreck had made a junction at Inverlochy, where they rounded up and killed some Macdonald stragglers. Argyll called up his chaplains to look at the grisly heap of dead: before the week was out he would have all Montrose's men stiff and stark as these.

It looked unpleasantly as though Argyll might be right. The Great Glen was sealed at both ends. In these desperate straits, desperate measures alone would serve. In the violent weather Argyll and Seaforth would expect Montrose to cower in the shelter of the glen and give battle as best he could. But suppose he defied both the weather and the mountains? Suppose he abandoned the glen and found some way back, through the pathless wilds, deep in drifted snow, skirting the forbidding rampart of Ben Nevis, and coming in over its shoulder to take Argyll by surprise at Inverlochy? He found a few shepherds of the Macdonalds of Keppoch who said they thought they could find a way. There were high passes, not easy to find even in summer, very difficult in the cold, the long winter nights and the snow. Montrose knew they must take the risk. Following the waters of the little river Tarff, black among the snows, he turned with his army into the mountains, and the driving blizzard blotted his tracks from sight. Seaforth's scouts and Argyll's scouts met in the middle of the Great Glen. Montrose and his army had vanished. The trap was empty.

But Montrose and his men were battling their cold and painful way through the mountains, through drifted snow, against the bitter wind. On the second day the weather cleared and a thaw set in, which did not much help matters, with every stream in spate. At night they struggled on by starlight. They had to keep going to keep warm. More than once they seemed to have lost their way. Many a glen in Lochaber has to this day its own legend of Montrose and claims that, on this epic march, he passed that way. Modern soldiers and historians, trying to follow his route in summer and in peace, have stood amazed at the daring which prompted and the skill which achieved what John Buchan has rightly called 'one of the great exploits in the history of British arms'.

On the second day the foremost men clashed with a party of scouting Campbells. They knew then that they were nearing Inverlochy, but they kept to the high ground and moved cautiously. As they crossed the lower spur of Ben Nevis, they saw in the glow of the winter dusk the castle of Inverlochy, the long arm of the sea-loch with Argyll's ship at anchor, and the camp-fires of the Campbell host glowing in the flat land round the castle. In spite of the cold, they lit no fires themselves. The Campbell scouts who had seen them took them to be a scattered band, and confirmed Argyll's belief that Montrose's army had disintegrated. They must, therefore, do nothing that would reveal the full size of their host. They froze, through the long winter night, warming themselves with the thought of the shock in store for the Campbells in the morning. The last of the oatmeal – their only food for many days past – was shared out for breakfast. They made a kind of cold porridge by pounding it with snow, and scooped it up on their dirks, Montrose with the rest.

Inverlochy Castle (The Royal Commission on the Ancient and Historical Monuments of Scotland)

One splendid formality he had insisted on retaining. Somehow, throughout that terrible march, in snow and wind, over rock and moor, they had carried with them the trumpet which had signalled the onset at Tippermuir and Aberdeen. No scattered group of Macdonalds would sound the attack with a trumpet, still less with the special fanfare reserved for occasions when the commander-in-chief was present. After their cold breakfast Montrose marshalled his men on the steep slope above Inverlochy in the winter dark. As the sun rose, the trumpet call would crack the clouds, and they would fall on the Campbells. Only when they heard the trumpet would the Campbells know who it was they had to face.

Argyll had slept on board his vessel in the sea-loch. By agreement with Auchinbreck, who bore command that day, he had planned to watch the fighting from the deck. No one at Inverlochy anticipated a serious action, even if the wandering band of Macdonalds did anything so foolhardy as to attack. The Campbells had been drawn up, in case of such an event, in the flat ground before Inverlochy. They were nearly four thousand strong and Auchinbreck had placed them in a solid square eight ranks deep. This was not the too long, too thin line that Montrose had broken at Tippermuir and Aberdeen. Besides, they were Highland troops, used to Highland fighting and burning to avenge recent disgrace to their clan.

At the sound of the trumpet the Macdonalds came down from the height like water bursting a dam; the mountainside was dark with their plaids and the air tingled with their blood-curdling war-cries. Auchinbreck galloped forward to steady his lines, but already the furious impact of the Macdonald charge had pushed back the first rank on to the second and the startled Campbells were trampling each other.

Auchinbreck might have rallied them yet, but suddenly a yell of triumph went up from the Macdonalds and an echoing cry of dismay from his own men. With the rapid, rhythmic splash of oars, Argyll's galley was speeding away down the loch. The Campbell chief had deserted his people for the second time.

Even so his troops fought on. Here and there in the confusion bands of Campbells rallied again and stood their ground sword in hand. 'They fought,' Montrose said afterwards, 'like men with a better cause.' But the fearful tale of slaughter – fifteen hundred dead – bore witness to their vain courage in defeat. A Catholic priest who followed the Irish and has left his own account of this wild campaign, walked among the Campbell dead and dying that night to give comfort where he could. The field, he wrote, was strange and sad to see, 'from the number of bodies of tall men, principally Campbells,' lying dead together. It was a disaster to the strength of the clan which thirty years could not make good. That day, 2 February 1645, long remained of evil memory.

The night after Inverlochy, after weeks of cold and wet and

continuous action, Montrose warmed his roughened hands at the fireside, cut himself a quill pen, and sat down to write his dispatch to the king. He had received many of the Campbell prisoners into mercy, he said; in general, they were loyal, being misled by their chief. He believed that there would be no more trouble from the clan. 'As to the state of affairs in this kingdom, the bearer will fully inform Your Majesty that, through God's blessing, I am in the fairest hopes of reducing this kingdom to Your Majesty's obedience. And if the measures I have concocted with your other loyal subjects fail me not, which they hardly can, I doubt not before the end of this summer I shall be able to come to Your Majesty's assistance with a brave army. . . . Only give me leave, after I have reduced this country to Your Majesty's obedience and conquered from Dan to Beersheba, to say to Your Majesty then, as David's general said to his master, "Come thou thyself lest this country be called by my name."'

CHAPTER SEVEN

HEROIC VENTURES

Four times Montrose and his happy few had faced and beaten the forces sent against him – at Tippermuir, Aberdeen, Fyvie and Inverlochy. The natural romance and gallantry of the Scots warmed to the story. In Edinburgh the mob raised a mock cheer for the fugitive Argyll when he came to Parliament with his arm in a sling 'as if he had been at bones breaking'. In taverns off the Canongate, at Perth, at Aberdeen, even at dourly Covenanting Dundee, genial toasts were raised to 'the gallant Graeme'.

In answer the government at Edinburgh had Montrose proclaimed a traitor and excommunicated by the Kirk. His coat of arms was publicly defaced in Parliament and henceforward all zealous Covenanters made a point of referring to him simply as 'James Graham'. This done, the government sent two messages to England, a blustering one to Parliament declaring that they had not lost more than thirty men at a petty little skirmish at Inverlochy, and an urgent one to Lord Leven imploring immediate help.

Baillie hurried to Aberdeen and stood on the defensive while Montrose marched up the Great Glen among the melting snows. From time to time he had to find messengers bold and skilful enough to undertake to carry his dispatches to England. They were not always lucky and those who were taken in Scotland were usually hanged. But William Rollo had got through to Oxford and been knighted by the king, and Tom Sydserf – nothing of a soldier but a born actor – also got through, disguised as a pedlar of religious tracts. One of these bold messengers was now sent to Aboyne at Carlisle, asking him to rejoin Montrose.

Before Aboyne could respond, Montrose received unexpected help from another of Huntly's sons. Lord Gordon, the eldest and the heir, joined him at Elgin with a contingent of cavalry drawn from the Gordon clan. Huntly himself, in spite of Montrose's letters and messages, held haughtily aloof. He was, in his peculiar fashion, unshakably loyal to the king, but he greatly resented the fact that Montrose, and not he, was Lieutenant-Governor of Scotland. It is conceivable, too, that he was jealous of the affection in which his two sons, Gordon and Aboyne, held Montrose.

Lord Gordon was about twenty-five, had served in France and was a soldier as competent as he was valiant. With all the fire of his race he had also a peculiar grace and gentleness, and he had been known, like Montrose, to try his hand at poetry. Common interests beyond the horizon of the war drew the two men together. Montrose would have been less than human had he not sometimes longed, during interminable evenings while Alasdair and his friends with bombastic braggadocio fought all their battles over again, for half an hour's talk with someone who had heard of Tasso and could discuss the rhyme scheme of a sonnet. George Gordon gave him this.

On Lord Gordon's side friendship soon passed into hero-worship. He would stand, people said, looking upon Montrose as one rapt. Should things go wrong, he used to say, he would follow him to the farthest mountains, to rocks and caves and the habitation of wolves.

Lord Gordon's young devotion came at a time when Montrose sorely needed it. In that same month his son John died. Little is known of the circumstances, but there cannot be much doubt of the cause. Whatever his father tried to do for him he could not much mitigate the rigours of those awful marches, and John, at fifteen, was probably the victim of physical exertions far beyond his strength.

No sooner did news of his death reach the Covenanters than a troop of horse swept down in a raid on the town of Montrose and carried off his younger brother James a prisoner to Edinburgh Castle.

Montrose had little time for private anxiety and sorrow. He had been ill with fever himself, but early March found him on his feet again and

George Gordon, 2nd Marquess of Huntly (National Galleries of Scotland)

ready to move against Baillie. An unexpected setback added to his difficulties, for Huntly, resentful and jealous, called his clan home. No order from his father and his chief would make Lord Gordon leave Montrose, but most of the cavalry went home. Thus once again Montrose was left hopelessly weak in this most valuable weapon of war. He could not openly challenge Baillie until he had more horse. There was nothing for it but to resort again to the tip-and-run tactics which had proved so successful in the previous year. First, he retreated into the Cairngorm massif to reappear with a threatening air well to the south of Aberdeen where Baillie least expected him. Thoroughly put out by this jack-in-the-box act, Baillie turned suspicious and, to the annoyance of his task-masters in Edinburgh, remained on the defensive in Aberdeen. He was still skulking when Montrose, with incredible effrontery, made a sudden raid on Dundee.

It was a town solid for the Covenant, out on the coast, separated from the Highlands not only by the low-lying coastal plain but by the additional barrier of the Sidlaw Hills, and it was nearly thirty miles away from Montrose's temporary headquarters at Dunkeld.

He took his cavalry – about a hundred and fifty in all - and six hundred selected foot, two hundred of them musketeers; they carried nothing but their arms. The baggage, such as it was, and all the rest of the foot, were instructed to follow the edge of the hills from Dunkeld to Brechin and wait there for the return of the Dundee party.

At midnight on a mild April night Montrose and his seven hundred and fifty left Dunkeld. At ten in the morning they were outside Dundee. By eleven o'clock they had taken the town.

Montrose had a clear purpose in this raid, besides that of frightening his enemies. He needed oatmeal and gunpowder, and these commodities the troops were instructed to search for as soon as the town was entered. They had been at work for about five hours when Montrose, who was watching from a hill just outside the town, was aware of a breathless scout approaching him. His information was

Plan of the Campaign of Dundee and Auldearn

simple, certain, and disastrous. A Covenanting force of about three thousand men was just a mile away.

Montrose's officers surrounded him with frantic and contradictory plans. The more professional urged him to flee at once with the cavalry, abandoning the foot soldiers in the town. Others, with greater chivalry and less experience, were for one last, hopeless, glorious charge – a hundred and fifty cavalry against three thousand, and death with honour for them all.

Montrose silenced them, which must have taken several minutes of their precious time. There would be no heroic, hopeless charge and no desertion of the infantry. While he hovered before the town with his horse, the rest of them would assemble the infantry and march them out of the town on the farther side. They were only a small force – six hundred; twenty minutes would be time enough to chivy them off the fleshpots and out of the town. 'Gentlemen,' he said, with a fine assumption of calm that he can hardly have felt, 'you do your duty; leave the issue to God, and the management to me.'

Somehow, they got the men together and out of the northern gate of the town as Baillie came up on the south. Montrose and the cavalry followed, guarding the rear. A well-directed fusillade from the musketeers discouraged the pursuers from following too close. After some anxious miles, night covered the retreat.

But Montrose's troubles were only beginning. He had been

compelled by the sudden surprise to get out of Dundee on any road he could, and here he was at nightfall making fast along the coast road, almost due east, towards Arbroath. General Baillie, who was no fool, would certainly occupy all the inland roads between them and the mountains. Montrose had got his men out of Dundee, but would he ever get them back into the Highlands?

They marched for two hours after dark, and then, having covered more than fifty miles that day, stopped, as they thought, for the night. But it was only until Montrose's scouts could give him word of the enemy's position. They had done exactly what Montrose feared. Baillie had taken up his position in the direct way from the coast to the mountains.

There is one thing that a pursuing force does not usually reckon on: that the retreating army will turn back in its tracks. Baillie had stationed troops at all the passable roads between Arbroath and the hills. He had stationed none on the coast road back to Dundee. Montrose saw the way out of the trap. In a pitch-black night his tired troops retraced their steps over the coast road, turned inland and skirted round between the garrison in Dundee and Baillie's main body sprawled across the Abroath-Brechin road. By dawn they were approaching the mountains, but so tired that they could not move a step farther. In the orchard of Careston Castle, which seemed to offer something in the way of defence, Montrose let them halt. They dropped in their tracks and slept where they lay, but only for two hours. Baillie's second-in-command, Colonel Hurry, had got wind of their movements and, full of amazement and rage, was in pursuit.

As his vanguard came in sight, Montrose's officers were still trying to rouse their men, with kicks, curses and blows. They got them to their legs half dizzy with sleep, while the cavalry, itself more dead than alive, and those of the musketeers who had any ammunition left, guarded the rear. Hurry came up only in time to see his prey vanishing into the misty distance of the mountains.

It had been a very near thing, but it had succeeded. Of all the achievements of Montrose it was this corkscrew retreat from Dundee which was most marvelled at and most admired by the military critics of the time.

A fortnight later Aboyne, the younger of Huntly's sons, at last rejoined Montrose with a handful of men he had brought from Carlisle. He and Gordon now decided to try a joint appeal to their father to send the fighting force of the clan to help Montrose. Their hurried mission was not wholly unsuccessful and they rejoined Montrose early in May 1645 with substantial reinforcements.

Colonel Hurry, however, who had been foiled at Dundee, was more astute and more daring than his commanding officer Baillie. He had tried with some skill to intercept the return of the Gordons so that Montrose had had to march rapidly down the Spey, out of his mountains, in order to meet them in the low-lying northern plain of Moray. Here Hurry, although Montrose chivied his rear all the way from Elgin to Inverness, had stolidly refused to be drawn into battle.

At Inverness he knew that he could expect reinforcements from the Frasers and the Mackenzies, who could usually be worked upon to side against the Gordons. It was now Montrose's turn to be anxious, for Hurry, with these Highland reinforcements, would be a very dangerous proposition. He decided to fall back immediately into the mountains. But Hurry, who lived up to his name, came after him so fast that he overtook him on the misty morning of 9 May at the hillocky little village of Auldearn, not far from Nairn and a mile or two from the coast.

The very uneven ground and the misty day were Montrose's only advantages. He placed Alasdair Macdonald with most of the infantry among a group of farm buildings on rising ground in front of Auldearn and put the Royal Standard in his keeping, so that Hurry would take this point for the centre and main body of his army. Montrose with the cavalry and the remaining infantry were stationed on a low ridge, partly masked by a copse, overlooking Auldearn. His intention was to

wait until Hurry was engaged with
Macdonald and then to bring in his
main force in a flank attack.

Hurry, baffled by the mist and the
confusing conformation of the hills and
ridges, fell into the trap, but unhappily
Alasdair Macdonald, contrary to all
orders, forsook his defensive position,
charged on Hurry's superior forces and
was all but overwhelmed.

In the mist Montrose could not see
what had happened, until a panting
messenger came running up the ridge to
tell him the Macdonalds were in flight.
Fortunately, he spoke too low for the
restive troops on the ridge to hear.
Montrose realized that all now depended

Plan of the Battle of Auldearn

on the Gordon cavalry charge and the Gordon morale. 'My lord,' he
shouted to George Gordon, 'Macdonald has routed the enemy. Shall we
stand by idle while he carries away the honour of the day?'

The Gordons needed no more encouragement. Through the mist,
down the damp slope, thundered Lord Gordon's cavalry on to Hurry's
flank. Montrose meanwhile, with the remaining foot, hastened under
cover of the ridge to see what had become of Alasdair. His troops were
not in flight; they had managed to make a stand in – of all places – a
row of pigsties, whose low walls gave them some cover. Alasdair
himself, gigantically strong, shattered the pikes of Hurry's advancing
infantry by presenting his Highland targe or shield to their points,
and cutting them off by three and four at a time when they were
driven into it. Montrose's timely coming gave the Macdonalds fresh
vigour. Meanwhile, Hurry's cavalry, confused by a mistaken order, and
startled by the unexpected descent of the Gordons out of the mist,

fled almost without fighting. His more valiant infantry thus had to withstand the Gordon attack on their unprotected flank while the Macdonalds and Montrose still held them in front. They fought doggedly but the mist and the ground told heavily against them, and Hurry found himself forced to extricate his men and get back to Inverness with what he could, leaving about a third of his forces dead or captured.

In Edinburgh the Committee of Estates in fear and anger discussed the military situation. Argyll had been defeated; Hurry had been defeated; Baillie was afraid to attack. What were they to do?

It was Huntly who temporarily saved the situation for them. For the second time he called the Gordon cavalry home. Lord Gordon in a burst of passion threatened to shoot any man who dared to go, but Montrose would not risk mortally offending Huntly or making civil strife within the clan. He overruled the angry young man and let the Gordons go.

The respite granted to the Covenanters was not a long one. Huntly relented within a month. Provided once more with cavalry Montrose had now only one objective, to bring Baillie to fight.

There followed, in the last fortnight of June, a game of hide-and-seek up and down the glens which run eastward from the central massif of Cairngorm to the coastal plain. Baillie could get some way up the rivers Dee, Don or Urie, but could not traverse the ground in between, which presented no difficulty to Montrose. Baillie manœuvred so as to get Montrose to fight in a place which suited his troops; Montrose counter-manœuvred to catch Baillie where it suited him. Early on the morning of 2 July Baillie crossed the Don at Bridge of Alford, thinking to cut off Montrose's retreat into the mountains. Montrose, getting wind of his movements, immediately occupied a ridge which dominated the river valley, taking care, however, to keep his troops for the most part out of sight behind the curve of the ridge while Baillie crossed the river. He now had his opponent below him in boggy

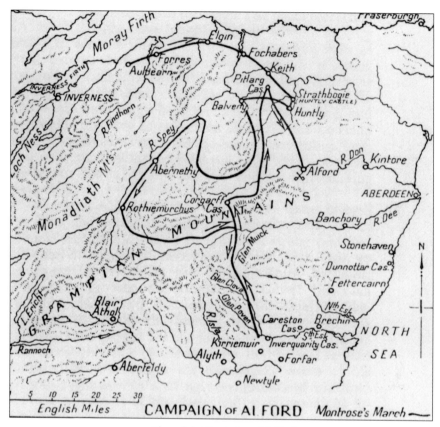

Plan of the Campaign of Alford

uneven ground with the river at his back, an awkward position in which he could not make the most of his numbers.

For once Montrose faced him in almost conventional order – infantry in the centre, and two hundred horse on each wing. Behind the infantry was a small reserve guarding the baggage, with a crowd of squabbling Gordon and Macdonald boys, a dozen carts and a number of Highland ponies. In charge of this unorthodox unit was young Archie Napier, Montrose's eighteen-year-old nephew. Lord Gordon was on the right wing, his brother Aboyne on the left.

The worst problem was Baillie's cavalry. He had a thousand to

The view from Reekie to the Bridge of Alford, the site of the Battle of Alford, 1644. Montrose's vantage position on Gallows Hill is off the picture to the right (Jim Henderson)

Montrose's four hundred, enough to hold the Gordon horse in play and to ride down Montrose's foot at the same time. He was foiled by the experienced ruthlessness of one of Montrose's best lieutenants, Nat Gordon, who ordered his men to use the brutal expedient of 'houghing' the horses, which meant going for their legs and bellies with their dirks.

These tactics broke the force of the cavalry attack on the infantry in the centre, and Lord Gordon, after making short work of his opponents on the right wing, came in to help them. Meanwhile, great excitement had broken out among the boys with the baggage. The truth was that Archie Napier, hardly more than a boy himself, was as disappointed as they were at being left in the rear. At the first possible moment he brought in his reserve, and the boys, mounted on their ponies, or on

foot, came hurtling to the help of
the infantry. In the general
confusion Baillie thought some
unexpected reserve of horse had
come up. He sounded the retreat.

The victory was complete. Baillie,
with the poor remnant of his army,
fled towards Aberdeen, then, with
bitter haste, to Perth. Thence he
sent to Edinburgh, saying nothing
but a general mobilization of the
southern shires could now stop
Montrose.

This battle at Alford was fought
on 2 July 1645. The following
Sabbath from every pulpit in the
south the ministers called the people
to repent of their sins. Not without cause did God from time to time
send a scourge upon his people – Assyrian or Midianite, the Persian,
the Roman, or the Turk – and now the accursed Graham.

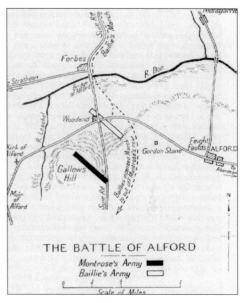

Plan of the Battle of Alford

But there was no rejoicing for the great victory at Alford in
Montrose's camp. George Gordon, just as the day was won, had been
killed by a stray bullet. His people, like the Greeks of old, had fought
to protect his body, and now they gathered round him, where he lay on
the trampled heather.

'Forgetting their victory and the spoil, they fixed their eyes upon the
lifeless body, kissed his face and hands, commended the singular beauty
of the corpse, compared the nobility of his descent with the
hopefulness of his parts, and counted that an unfortunate victory that
had stood them in so much. And truly their excess of sorrow for the
loss of this noble gentleman had conquered the conquerors, had they
not comforted themselves with the presence and safety of Montrose.

Nor could he refrain from himself bewailing with salt tears the sad and bitter fate of his most dear friend.' So wrote Montrose's chaplain, Wishart.

A few days later Montrose followed his coffin in solemn procession to its resting place in Aberdeen Cathedral. So, in the flower of his youth and the hour of victory, died Lord Gordon. Among Montrose's captains, he was fortunate.

CHAPTER EIGHT

TRIUMPH

The tale of Montrose's victories had lasted without intermission for eleven months. The time had come for him to leave the mountains and do what he had long planned – cross the Forth and invade the lowlands. Here he believed, with cause, there were many who would rise for the king.

Swift as his marches so often were, rapidly as he could decide and act in a crisis, he was not a reckless general. He made his preparations with care. First, he sent Aboyne to Speyside to raise more cavalry. While waiting for these, he marched into Angus where his cousin, Black Pate, had for some weeks been raising men among the Grahams. He was joined there by a number of chiefs with their following. Some like Clanranald, Glengarry, the MacNabs and the Atholl Stewarts had been with him in the previous autumn; others were newcomers, among them the Macleans, a great number of the broken clan of MacGregors and all Montrose's old friends and neighbours, Lord Airlie's kin, the Ogilvies.

Montrose now marched to the south-eastern borders of the Highlands, and for several days camped in Methven wood, not far from Perth. Below him Baillie's dispirited forces were guarding the town to which the Scottish Parliament had fled because of the plague raging in Edinburgh. When they saw the 'bloody

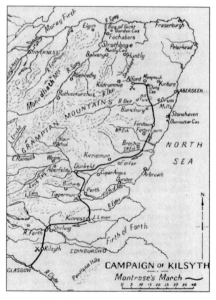

Plan of the Campaign of Kilsyth

murderer and excommunicate traitor James Graham' riding along the edge of Methven wood in broad daylight, as unconcerned as if Baillie were a hundred miles away, they may well have preferred the plague for companion.

Montrose did not attack. His action was a demonstration merely. When he withdrew, Baillie with a great air of bravado went and occupied Methven wood, to cheer up his troops and show them that they could do as well as Montrose. But they were not much cheered.

By this time Aboyne had come back with two hundred horse and three hundred foot. The Ogilvies, too, had brought in some cavalry. Montrose's numbers were never likely to be more satisfactory while he remained in the Highlands. Now or never, he must cross the Forth.

Following his usual policy of war by shock, Montrose marched direct to Kinross on the border of Fife, where the Covenanters were hurriedly recruiting. Here he paused just long enough for rumours of his nefarious intentions to permeate the district and upset the recruiting plans of his enemies, before turning west and following the Forth to Stirling. As he had hoped, the great men of the district gave him welcome and he was feasted at Alloa by the Earl of Mar.

Meanwhile, the Fifeshire men, unwillingly brought to arms, had been added to Baillie's forces, which numbered in all something over four thousand, with at least a thousand cavalry. With this substantial strength they followed after Montrose. They hoped at first to catch him at Stirling if he tried to rush the bridge. But he made a circuit to the north, to avoid trouble with the garrison, and crossed the Forth at a ford, left unguarded, five miles above the town.

The enemy came hurrying after him, for every effort must be made to prevent his entering Glasgow as he had entered Perth, Aberdeen and Dundee. Baillie would gladly have headed him away from Glasgow without fighting if possible but Argyll, who joined the army at Stirling, insisted that the time had come to annihilate James Graham in pitched battle.

Montrose had marched across the Campsie Hills, a low blunt range, covered with sparse, coarse pasture and stretches of moor. They followed him, sweating in the sultry August weather. Montrose was waiting for them on the farther side, just above the little village of Kilsyth. He had taken up a defensible position on cultivated ground, transected with low stone walls which served for breastworks. Between him and Baillie was a steep hollow. Baillie drew up his forces on the rising ground opposite and once more advised Argyll not to fight.

The heat was oppressive, and the well-dressed Lowlanders were stifling in their heavy clothes. Montrose had ordered his men to fight in their shirts (if they had them), an example which he and most of his officers followed. The unconventional spectacle of an army in white linen seems to have been the final exasperation to Argyll and the more vehement Covenanting leaders. They overruled Baillie and insisted on fighting.

They did worse, for they disapproved of Baillie's dispositions and rashly undertook to alter them in full view of the vigilant Montrose, who could hardly believe his eyes when he saw that they were attempting nothing less than a flank march across his front in broad daylight. He would have drawn more advantage from this fantastic situation, however, if the Macdonalds, enraged by the skirmishing of an insubordinate Covenanting officer, had not allowed themselves to be tempted too soon into one of their famous charges. Baillie's troops were in considerable disorder but they far outnumbered the Highlanders who were soon in great danger of being surrounded and cut off. But for once Montrose had a reasonable force of cavalry at his disposal. He turned to Airlie, the stout-hearted, white-haired old gentleman who had followed him

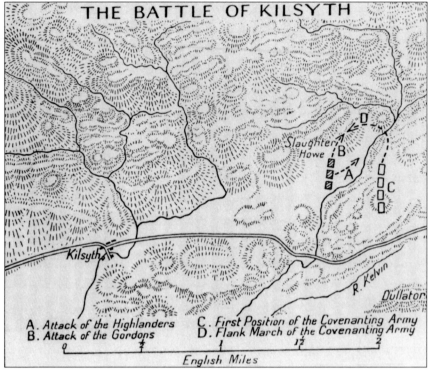

Plan of the Battle of Kilsyth

through every danger. 'My Lord,' he said, 'we look to the Ogilvies', and added for his old friend's especial ear: 'They yonder have engaged themselves too far by the foolhardiness of their youth; it is for the discretion of age to set it right.'

Airlie needed no more encouragement. His men were fresh, well-mounted and spoiling to show their valour. The shock of their impact broke one wing of the enemy horse, and drove them in on their own infantry. Their confusion was sufficient for Montrose to think that the rest of his infantry could abandon the defensive. At the impact of this second charge, Baillie's foot began to give. Argyll turned and fled with all the speed of his thoroughbred horse. The bad example was followed by the entire Covenanting cavalry. The infantry gave up the unequal struggle; some surrendered, some threw down their arms and ran. Montrose was master of the field. By the evening of that day, 18 August 1645, he was master of Scotland. After this Battle of Kilsyth, nothing that could be called an army remained in the country. Argyll fled to Berwick, where he was joined by the Chancellor Loudoun, and several other lords and leaders of the party. Others, more timorous still, took ship for Ireland.

Glasgow sent to invite the mercy of the victor. Young Napier and Nat Gordon, with a troop of horse, received the humble submission of Edinburgh. The doors of the Tolbooth were thrown open, and Montrose's friends were brought out with obsequious apologies. Their condition was shocking. Afraid of the plague, the gaoler of the Tolbooth had locked up his charges and left the town some time before. Since then they had had no water and no food save what could be passed in through the gratings by charitable people. Their clothes were filthy and in rags. They had had no beds or bedding but the bare boards, and the rats which infested the prison had attacked them while they slept.

From being the most abject and neglected of men, they became in twenty-four hours the most courted and cherished. The provost and bailies of Edinburgh escorted them home, kissing their gaunt, grimy hands and imploring them to say a good word for Edinburgh to the great and glorious Montrose.

The defeated party had good reason to fear the vengeance of Montrose. They had persistently refused to grant his men the ordinary rights of war. They had hanged or dirked the prisoners and executed any of Montrose's messengers whom they happened to take. They had imposed crippling fines on all his relations, seized his estates and imprisoned all his friends on whom they could lay hands, down to the seventeen-year-old wife of young Archie Napier.

For all the past months Montrose, in answer, had made it a point of honour to treat his prisoners well. He lodged them at Blair Castle with

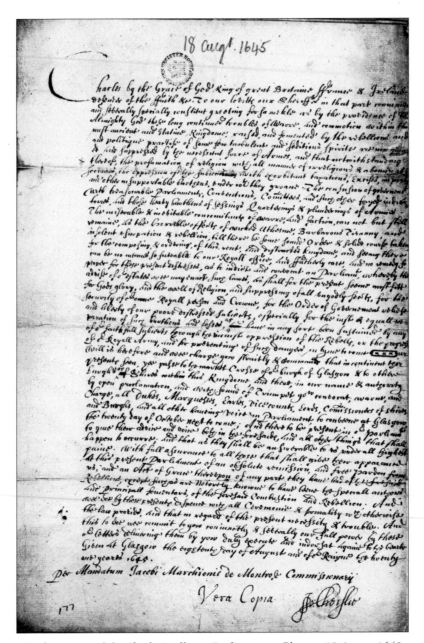

Proclamation made by Charles I calling a Parliament at Glasgow, 18 August 1645, spoken at Glasgow by Montrose (Scottish Record Office PA7/23/2/34)

as much comfort and dignity as the place would provide, allowed them to write to their friends and entertained them at his own table when he passed through.

His conduct during the three weeks which followed Kilsyth reflected the same high political ideals. The citizens of Edinburgh and Glasgow expected nothing less than that Scotland's two greatest cities would be handed over to the Highlanders to sack at will – a disaster which from time immemorial had been the Lowlanders' nightmare. But Edinburgh saw none of Montrose's army except the troop of horse which accepted the city's submission, and although he made a formal and triumphant entry to Glasgow, he kept his troops well in hand. At the first sign of disorder among the Highlanders he moved them out of temptation's way to Bothwell, where he set up his headquarters.

There was no penalization, no arrests – no demands for money even. For the past two years the good people of the south had been taxed to support their own army. They learned to their surprise that Montrose's troops fought without pay, needing none for the kind of lives they led. Furthermore, they did not even want much shelter. There was very little requisitioning of quarters for they preferred to sleep out, wrapped in their plaids, on the ground.

It would be going too far to say that none of the Highlanders took anything, for the good wives of the district certainly missed a chicken here and a cockerel there, and the washing off the line might be spirited away; but there was no violence and no thieving that Montrose and his officers could prevent. Compared even to their own troops, the common people found Montrose's men less burdensome. Montrose himself had taken temporary possession of Hamilton's mansion, Bothwell Palace. Hither, in unceasing stream, came the lords and gentry from all the south of Scotland, the loyalists to offer their services, and the Covenanters their apologies. He received them all and proclaimed a pardon to all who laid down arms and swore allegiance to the king.

*Bothwell Castle (The Royal Commission on the Ancient and Historical Monuments
of Scotland)*

Old Lord Napier, Airlie and his son Lord Ogilvie were sometimes doubtful. They pointed out to Montrose that he was dealing, in many cases, with notoriously dishonest men. Montrose was as well aware of the dangers as they were. But what was the alternative? To seize a score of the worst and send them prisoners to the Highlands? Actions such as these would increase the bitterness of Scottish politics, which it was his ambition to mitigate. He may have been wrong to be steadfast to his ideal, but in an age of vindictive cruelty, it is much to his honour that he was so.

Montrose hoped above all that the king, on whom he had from the first urged moderation, would support him in this policy. A few days after Kilsyth he received letters from Charles which gratified all his desires. The king wrote that he had absolute confidence in his

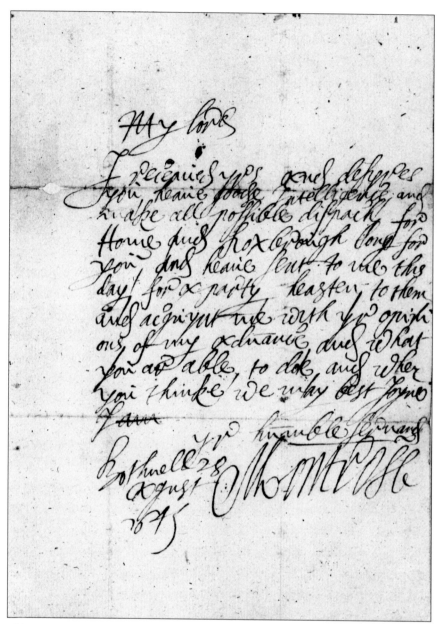

Montrose to Lord Ogilvie, 28 August 1645, on a rendezvous for the invasion of England (on loan to the Scottish Record Office, GD1/54/7)

Lieutenant-Governor of Scotland, in token of which he sent him a signed and sealed commission to call a new Parliament, over which he gave him full powers to preside.

The war, as Montrose well knew, was by no means over. Since the king's disastrous defeat at Naseby in June of that year, all his hopes were fixed on the help that could be given him out of Scotland.

The maintenance of Montrose's power depended on the strength he could raise in the south. Recruiting in the southern parts of Scotland would take a good deal longer and require much more organization than it did in the Highlands. At Bothwell, he was extracting promises of help from all the southern lords and gentlemen, offers of a hundred foot here and of fifty horse there, so that little by little an army would come into being. He may not have believed all the promises, but he probably believed rather more than he should have done. Even so he did not imagine that he would have manned the south and made it safe for the king until the autumn.

There was another problem. The southern troops would not fight without pay. That meant a vote of money from the people; Montrose accordingly called a new Parliament at Glasgow for the middle of October.

In the midst of so much planning and organization he allowed himself and his army one day of formal glory. In the presence of hundreds of his new and supposed allies he reviewed the small army which had achieved so much. 'In a short and stately address,' as his chaplain, George Wishart, tells us, he thanked them in the king's name for what they had done. Then he called forward Alasdair Macdonald and, while the gigantic young Irishman knelt before him, gave him the accolade.

This was not the least glorious moment in a glorious day. If Caesar and Alexander had been in Montrose's mind on campaign, here on this field of martial pageantry, his thoughts may have gone to the days of ancient chivalry, when knighthood was the reward of valour in battle, and one true knight could bestow the honour on another.

What he and his friends had done was as much the outcome of tenacity and well-organized purpose as of valour alone. But on this August day of 1645, Montrose may have been, as his critics said of him, living 'as in a romance'. It would be a harsh critic who would grudge him at such a time, with his friends about him and his banners crowned with victory, one day that would shine through dark years ahead, lit with poetic glory.

CHAPTER NINE

DISASTER

The day after the review Montrose sent Sir Alasdair Macdonald towards Galloway and Kintyre to recruit. Now that the momentary glory was over, he had much reason for anxiety. The king's cause in England was desperate and Charles, of course, could see the problem only from his own angle. General David Leslie, who had recently succeeded Lord Leven as the commander of the Scots army in England, had abandoned his English allies at a moment's notice and was hurrying by forced marches up to the Scottish border. Charles argued that the sooner Leslie could be put out of action, the better. Let Montrose, therefore, wipe out Leslie and then bring help to Charles in England.

General David Leslie (National Galleries of Scotland)

Montrose was very willing to wipe out Leslie, but he could only do so by his usual tactics: by drawing him up towards the mountains, tiring him, puzzling him, and finally pouncing on him. This would take several weeks, even if Leslie were less wary than Montrose conceived him to be. The other alternative was to wait on the defensive until the promised Lowland troops joined him, and then to attack Leslie with superior, or at least equal forces. But it would be dangerous to the point of folly to march against Leslie with only the small force at present under his command.

Yet this was what Charles, from the distance of England, very peremptorily demanded.

While Montrose hesitated two of the greatest Border lords, Roxburgh and Home, promised him two thousand men within a week, if he would come to the Border in person. Feeling that these two at least were trustworthy, Montrose, not very willingly, agreed. On Thursday 4 September he marched from Bothwell, with seven hundred Highland infantry, commanded in Alasdair's absence by his lieutenant, Seumas O'Cahan, and by two hundred horse, mostly from Stirlingshire and Angus. He would have had larger forces, but all the Gordon contingent, horse and foot, had gone back overnight to the Highlands. Montrose was realizing too late that Napier and Airlie had been right to warn him against some of the gentry he had received at Bothwell. Agents of Argyll's had undoubtedly mingled with his soldiers and stirred up the latent jealousies of the clans, working even on Aboyne himself to think he was doing neither Huntly nor the Gordons any service by fighting to increase the glory of Montrose.

On Saturday 6 September, Montrose heard at Cranston the disquieting news that Leslie had reached Berwick and was marching up the east coast with the evident intention of getting between him and the Highlands.

He decided, none the less, to go on towards the Border, join with the promised forces of Roxburgh and Home, and then give chase to Leslie. The next day, he was a little encouraged by a message from Lord Traquair, who owned wide lands not far from Selkirk. He sent his eldest son with a troop of a hundred horse which he begged Montrose to accept as a personal bodyguard and added that he would himself keep Montrose informed of all Leslie's movements.

Montrose marched on to Kelso where he had fixed his rendezvous with Roxburgh and Home. Here he received his first really bad news. Roxburgh and Home, coming up with fifteen hundred horse, had had the misfortune to run into Leslie's second in command, Middleton. He

Plan of the Campaign of Philiphaugh

had greeted them cheerfully thinking that they had come to join him. Making the best of a bad job, for he outnumbered them, they had pretended that this was indeed their intention. Off they had gone with him to Berwick.

There was now nothing left for Montrose to do but give up this futile southward march and hurry back to his base near Glasgow. Turning west from Kelso, he entered Selkirk with his cavalry on the night of 12 September. The Irish foot camped a few miles farther up the Yarrow at Philiphaugh. According to Traquair's information there were no enemy troops nearer than Berwick; they could rely on a quiet night.

At midnight Montrose was disturbed by the sound of horses. Young Traquair and his hundred men were stealthily leaving. Leslie, as Lord Traquair well knew, had long since turned round in his march to the Highlands. He was even now at Philiphaugh and had surrounded Montrose's infantry. In the early hours of a misty September morning Montrose and the cavalry galloped up the Yarrow to the rescue. But Leslie had about six thousand troops, of whom two thousand were cavalry and all Montrose's efforts to relieve his doomed infantry were in vain.

Here, as at Dundee, but with greater haste and anguish, his older officers gave Montrose the only possible council – if every man set spurs to his horse and fended for himself they might escape singly, thus saving at least some of the cavalry, and Montrose's own life. But Montrose answered them as the chivalrous hot-heads had done at Dundee. He

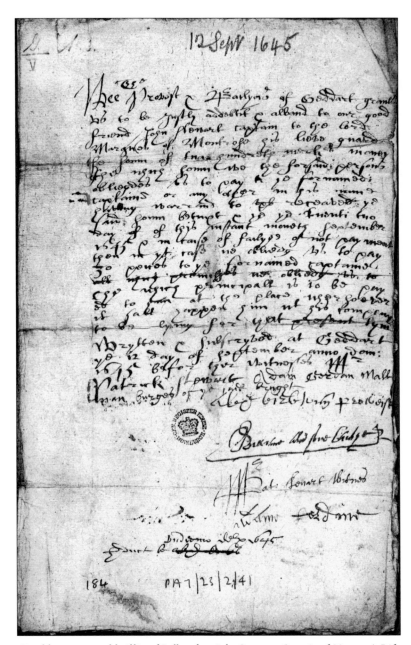

Bond by provost and baillies of Jedburgh to John Stewart, Captain of Montrose's Life Guard, for 200 merks, 12 September 1645 (Scottish Record Office, PA7/23/2/41)

Newark Castle was the scene of the massacre of scores of Montrose's Irish troops after the Battle of Philiphaugh (Humphrey Household)

would not abandon the infantry or leave the field, nor should anyone take him alive. In the mist and confusion all orders were vain and all ranks equal. His friends got hold of his horse's bridle and forced him to go.

The infantry, seeing that all was lost, raised the white flag. Leslie and Middleton were not bloodthirsty. They promised the men their lives if they laid down their arms, and the Macdonalds marched out of their stone-walled enclosure, piling up their swords and muskets as they went. Then Leslie, as was his unpleasant duty, explained the terms to his council of war on which the ministers sat with the officers. One and all the ministers condemned the terms. In cold blood the disarmed prisoners were put to the sword. The officers were reserved for formal execution later.

Great was the jubilation among the Covenanting leaders at the news of Philiphaugh, but it did not last for long. Less than a fortnight later Montrose, with a new force of about fifteen hundred men recruited in Atholl, took up his quarters at Buchanan Castle, whence he could threaten Glasgow. He hoped that before the winter came he would be able to bluff Leslie into fighting and so redeem his defeat. But the strong enchantment which his unbroken series of victories had worked against his enemies was broken at last. Leslie would not allow himself to be manœuvred into battle.

One misfortune now followed fast upon another. Alasdair Macdonald withdrew his help. He had come into Scotland to fight the Campbells for Kintyre and, after his great year with Montrose, he seems to have felt that he had given as much of his time and services to the king as honour and duty required. Marching ferociously up and down Kintyre and wasting the Campbell lands, he remained deaf to Montrose's plea that he should come back to the main body.

Montrose had also lost many of his best officers on the flight from Philiphaugh, Lord Ogilvie, Nat Gordon and Sir William Rollo had been taken prisoner. For a long time the standard-bearer, Hay of Dalgetty, was also missing. But he rejoined Montrose at Buchanan, after many wanderings, with the standard safe.

While Leslie held Glasgow against Montrose, Argyll and the triumphant party demonstrated their grisly power within its walls. On those very days of October, when Montrose had hoped to preside over a free Scots Parliament, his captured followers were condemned to death. This barbarous procedure against prisoners of war was described as 'purging the land from blood-guiltiness'.

Lord Ogilvie escaped the night before his execution by the ingenuity of his sister who took his place in prison. The rest died on the scaffold. Among the victims were three boys of barely eighteen. When the last of these young heads fell under the axe, one of the attendant ministers rubbed his hands and said: 'The work gangs bonnily on.' The abominable saying became proverbial.

The officers of the Macdonalds who had been spared were also brought to trial. O'Cahan was hanged 'on a long tow' over the castle wall of Edinburgh. Another of their captains was transported to Perth to make an example there; on the way his honourable captor Middleton, sickened by the vile business, let him escape. He rejoined Montrose, breathing fire and vengeance.

Montrose now faced a new problem. He still had, at Blair, a number of distinguished prisoners. His soldiers implored him to pay blood with blood and put these men to death. He refused to do so. Let others break their terms; gentlemen who carried the king's commission must keep their honour bright. 'If the meanest corporal in my army had given quarter to their general,' he said, 'I would abide by it.'

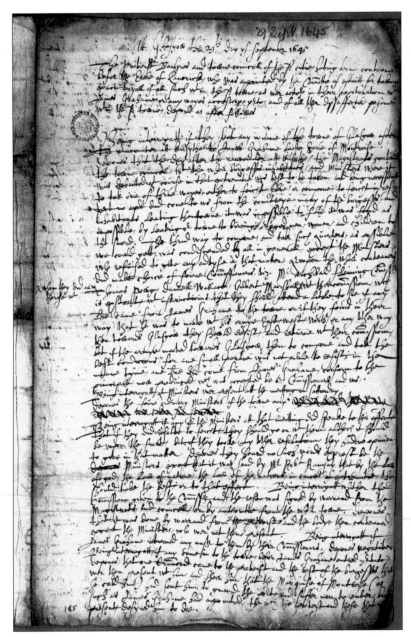

Above and opposite: Deposition by the provost, baillies and council of Glasgow before the Earl of Lanark as to their dealings with Montrose, 29 September 1645 (Scottish Record Office, PA7/23/2/42)

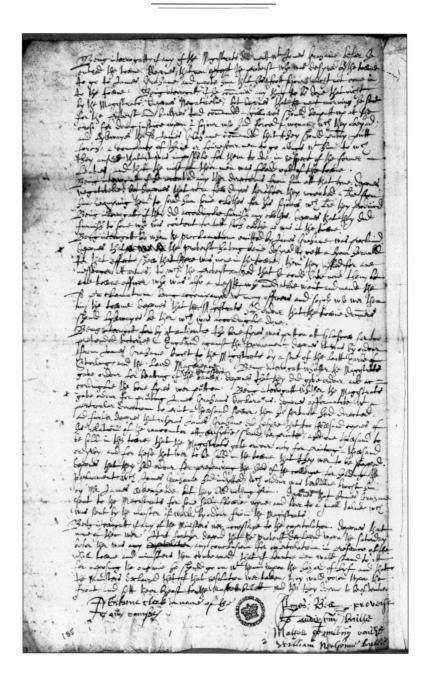

In November he went once more up the Spey to get help from the Gordons. They gave him none. The jealous Huntly saw in Montrose's defeat his own chance of becoming the king's sole champion. He suddenly remembered a commission, granted him three years before, of which he had, to his shame, made little use until this time. On the strength of this he gathered his clan for some private operations of his own, which he represented as important Royalist manœuvres.

Montrose had failed with the Gordons but, by much diplomacy and persuasion, he brought in the Frasers, the Mackenzies and some other of the northern clans. By the end of March 1646 he could count on a force of nearly five thousand from the region round Inverness. His strenuous efforts to take the town itself failed chiefly because Huntly refused to cooperate.

Meanwhile, Black Pate had manfully done his part in Atholl, drawing together nearly a thousand men. On their way to join Montrose they ran into a small regiment of Campbells, almost Argyll's last, at Callander, and scattered them in a brief skirmish.

Less fortunate was young Napier whom Montrose had sent to fortify his own Kincardine Castle. Middleton brought heavy ordnance against it and damaged, not the walls, but the water supply at his first cannonade. This compelled the garrison to surrender after a fortnight's thirsty resistance. Young Napier himself escaped, but the castle was fired and mined. Nothing was left of Montrose's home but a shapeless wreck of fallen masonry.

Yet, all things considered, the situation by the spring of 1646 was almost hopeful. There was substantial support in the north and, but for the Gordons, in most of the central Highlands. Leslie had had to go back to England with the bulk of his army to fulfil Scotland's treaty obligations to Parliament. Only Middleton was in the field against Montrose. Colonel Hurry – the most surprising and most helpful sign of all – had thrown up his commission with the Covenanters and joined Montrose's staff.

*Kincardine Castle was positioned on the Howe of Mearns plain below the hill-line in the centre
of the picture; it was demolished in 1646 (Jim Henderson)*

His plans were ripening for the spring campaign when he received
news which paralysed all further action. King Charles had surrendered
to the Scots army in England.

The king had taken this course because the Covenanters were
quarrelling with their English Parliamentary allies. Parliament had
bought help from the Scots by agreeing to enforce Presbyterianism in
England. But during the war a new force had grown up in the
Parliamentary army, the so-called Independents, who refused to accept
any organized Church. Parliament was thus painfully embarrassed by
the demands of its own army on the one side and of the Presbyterian
Scots on the other. Here was evidently a situation of which the king
might have made good use. Charles grasped the possibilities but he

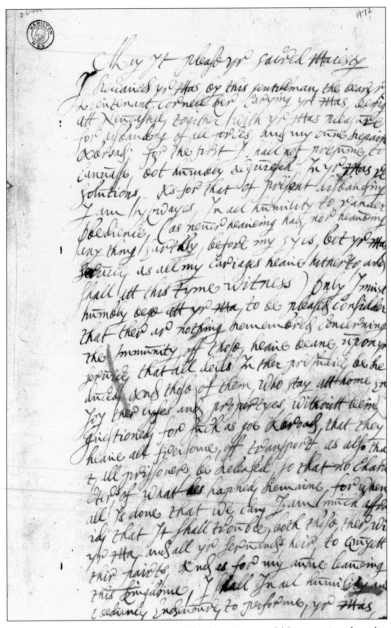

Above and opposite: Montrose's letter to Charles I, 2 June 1646, concerning the order to disband his forces and repair abroad (Scottish Record Office, GD406/1/1972)

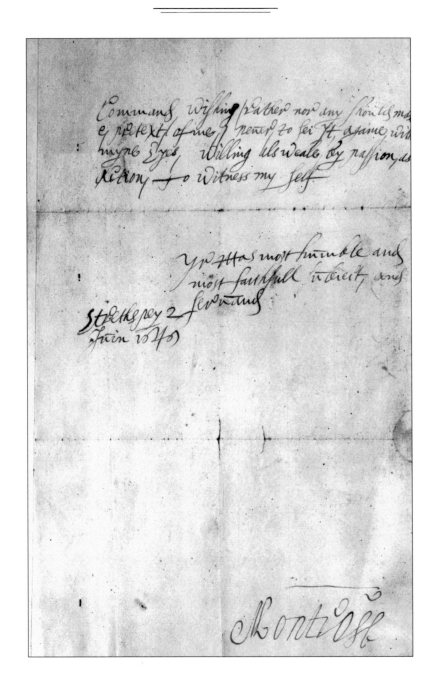

lacked the ability to exploit them. He had not, in the first place, reckoned on the single-minded ruthlessness of the Covenanters into whose hands he now so rashly delivered himself.

The first thing that they exacted of him was the repudiation of Montrose. Charles, who had fatally re-admitted Hamilton to favour, agreed to order Montrose to disband. This was a terrible error, for Montrose, still undefeated in the Highlands, was the one effective weapon still in Charles's hands. But the king, fated, as always, to trust his enemies and not his friends, believed that he could win the support of Argyll by abandoning Montrose.

Montrose, who saw at once the full extent of the king's error, was at first convinced that Charles was acting under compulsion. But when Charles twice confirmed the order, and Montrose's hard-won allies, discouraged by the king's surrender, began to drift away, he had no choice but to appoint a meeting with Middleton to make terms. His forces were large enough for him to exact good terms – if they were kept. He himself and most of his principal supporters undertook to leave the country not later than the end of August. Transport was to be provided by the Covenanters. All the rest had permission to return unmolested to their homes without loss of land, fines or other injury.

Late in July he took his last farewell of his remaining troops on Speyside, thanking them in brief and simple words for their services. They had done what they could, but the king had chosen another way and they must submit. He had difficulty in persuading them to disband; they crowded round him, kissing his hands with tears and imploring him to keep them with him, in the remote parts of Scotland, beyond seas, anywhere. They would follow him to the ends of the earth, 'a general so valiant, so skilful and so much beloved'.

It could not be. Slowly they dispersed to their homes. In those days, in his dwindling camp by the Spey, he must have written more than one note of recommendation for a departing officer. That which he gave to Black Pate has survived – a melancholy letter of credit drawn on a future which never came.

> Whereas Patrick Graham younger of Inchbrakie has been employed by us in His Majesty's service and has approved himself most faithful and valiant in everything, still as he was commanded by us, these are therefore not only to witness the same but also to assure him (whensover it shall please God to render His Majesty's service into the former condition and restore unto His Majesty his just rights) that, in His Majesty's name and authority, he shall be thankfully acknowledged and bountifully rewarded according as he has gallantly deserved. Given at Strathspey 25 July 1646.

When the last had gone, those doomed to exile made their sad way to the coast to wait for the promised shipping. They waited not far from old Montrose, where his home had been, and his father-in-law's house at Kinnaird where his children were. It is uncertain whether he was able to see them.

Some months earlier his wife Magdalen, in a petition to that very Parliament which was daily condemning her husband's friends to the gallows and the block, had asked to be made guardian of her three children. It was perhaps natural for a mother to address such a petition to her husband's enemies. But Argyll's party, who only a few months before had sent a troop of horse to seize her eldest son, would hardly have granted the request had they not believed that Montrose's children in their mother's care would be removed from their father's influence. They granted her request without the least hesitation; the action speaks for itself. It is the last *historic* fact in the obscure story of Magdalen.

An ancient legend does, however, add one mitigating word, which may be true. That year Magdalen fell ill; with fear, anxiety and a

Magdalen, Lady Montrose (Private Collection)

divided heart, she had cause enough. Montrose, from afar off, heard that his wife was dying, and cut his way through enemy country with a troop of horse, to follow her coffin to the grave.

So far the legend. But the true story of Montrose's wife remains a mystery. Certainly she died at about this time, but we do not know how, or where, or when.

Meanwhile, no ships came for Montrose and his friends. When at last, on 31 August, a vessel arrived, the surly captain said that she must stay in port for three days' repairs. The jaws of the trap were closing; after midnight that night, Montrose and his friends could by rights be arrested for exceeding the limit allowed them. At Stonehaven Montrose found the captain of a Norwegian ship and offered him gold to take them off. The Norwegian could not take them all. Montrose sent the others on board and himself stayed behind.

He rode through the night to Montrose with one of his chaplains. Here, for safety, he put on a shabby black suit, and carrying the chaplain's unpretentious baggage, in the guise of his servant, got a passage on a small fishing boat. A week later he landed in Bergen, empty-handed and heavy-hearted.

CHAPTER TEN

EXILE AND RETURN

Montrose was in Germany when he heard that Argyll's party, unable to come to terms with the king, had handed him over to his English enemies. To his proud and loyal heart this cold-blooded betrayal of the king by his countrymen was a cruel wound; he felt that the honour of Scotland had been soiled.

The king himself protested that he had been sold, a phrase to which Argyll and his party objected. They had merely agreed – so they said – to evacuate the town of Newcastle, their English headquarters, in return for the payment of their army. They had had to leave Charles behind, and it was nothing to do with them if the English had taken him over along with the town.

The blood money, as the Royalists persisted in calling it, did not all go to the army. Argyll received £30,000. So did Hamilton, who claimed his share as an indemnity for the damage that, according to him, Montrose had done to his house and lands.

Montrose at once offered to organize a new invasion of Scotland. But the queen, who from her impoverished court in Paris chiefly directed the projects of the exiled Royalists, was not encouraging. He did not, however, cease to consider this possibility, keeping in touch with Prince Rupert, Prince Maurice and all the more active of king Charles's followers. Even at this time of deepest anxiety and gloom, he had not outgrown his youth; for the code names he used in this correspondence show that he partly saw the characters of his contemporaries in terms of the romances he had read as a boy. Hamilton is 'Captain Luckless', Argyll the 'Ruling Elder', and he himself – cast for the hero's part – is 'Venture Fair'.

Yet there was more practical good sense than romanticism in his plans. It was possible in those days for a distinguished soldier to get permission to raise and keep in being a private army, or rather the skeleton staff of an army, so as to be ready in case of war. This was what Montrose now set out to do, in preparation for the moment when his king should call on him.

His reputation in Europe stood very high. His extraordinary achievements were widely known through the Latin account of them recently composed and published by his chaplain George Wishart. This book was not only popular in France and the Low Countries. It was also well known in England and Scotland, in spite of official efforts to discredit it under the disparaging nickname of *Montrose's Fairy Tales*.

But his own charm and dignity did him as much good in the cultured courts of Europe as Wishart's book. Cardinal de Retz had put it on record that when he met him in Paris he thought him 'the only man in the world who has ever brought to my mind such heroes as we read of in the pages of Plutarch'. He became within a few months a Marshal of France, and a Marshal of the Holy Roman Empire, with permission to recruit in the imperial dominions.

While foreign princes recognized his worth, his own unhappy sovereign stumbled blindly once again into the fatal orbit of Hamilton. Hamilton was chiefly responsible for the lamentable scheme known as 'the Engagement' in which king Charles involved himself while he was a prisoner of the English Army at Hampton Court. This was an ill-conceived plot on the part of a faction of the Covenanters (but not Argyll) to invade England in the summer of 1648 in conjunction with a rising of the English Royalists.

Under competent military leadership something might have come of this. But Hamilton, who crossed the Border preceded by six trumpeters in scarlet, lost half his army in a running fight with Cromwell on the Lancashire moors, and the other half surrendered at Uttoxeter. A small stout major later reported to Parliament that as he

I. G.

DE REBUS

Auspiciis Sereniffimi, &
Potentiffimi

CAROLI

DEI Gratiâ Magnæ Britanniæ,
Franciæ & Hiberniæ REGIS, &c.

Sub imperio illuftriffimi JACOBI Mon-
tifrofarum Marchionis, Comitis
de Kincardin, &c.

Supremi Scotiæ Gubernatoris Anno
CIƆIƆCXLIV, *& duobus fequentibus præ-*
clarè geftis,

Commentarius.

Interprete A. S.

ANNO DOMINI CIƆIƆCXLVII.

The title page from George Wishart's book on Montrose, 1647 (The Trustees of
the National Library of Scotland)

entered Uttoxeter a large, splendidly dressed and breathless Scot had offered him his Garter jewel, imploring quarter and asserting his name was Hamilton.

So ended the military career of Captain Luckless, and with it king Charles's last hope of freedom and life.

Montrose was in Brussels raising men when, early in February, he heard the news of King Charles's execution. The shock stunned him; he fell down – dead, as George Wishart and his attendants first thought. But it was only a momentary swoon. When he came to himself he shut himself in his study alone for two days and nights. During that long solitary wrestling the whole of his political life must have passed before him. Now that the king was dead, all criticism of his policy or his judgement, let alone of his treatment of Montrose, was extinguished for ever. As he went over the past he must have seen with unutterable grief the logical steps by which the first revolt in Scotland had led to

The execution of Charles I (Ashmolean Museum, Oxford)

the final tragedy of the king's murder. That murder he must now either revenge or expiate.

Later, George Wishart found among the scribbled papers on his desk a scrap of poetry, Montrose's epitaph on the murdered king. He copied it out and showed it to other Royalists. In manuscript or by word of mouth it found its way to many a Royalist home. It was set to music twice in the next ten years, once by Samuel Pepys. Often enough the author remained unknown to those who treasured the lines. They became the anonymous, universal resistance poem of the Royalists during the terrible years which lay ahead.

Great, good and just, could I but rate
My grief and thy too rigid fate,
I'd weep the world in such a strain
As it should deluge once again.
But since thy loud-tongued blood demands supplies
More from Briareus' hands than Argus' eyes,
I'll sing thy dirge with trumpet sounds
And write thine epitaph with blood & wounds.

Three weeks later he kissed the hand of the new king at The Hague. Charles II was eighteen years old, a swarthy, black-eyed young man, the age that John would have been had he lived. Montrose placed before him at once his previously rejected plan to launch an invasion of Scotland, raise the Highlands and reconquer the country as he had done five years before. Charles II, still half-dazed by his father's death, and deeply moved at Montrose's offer, instantly made him out a Commission as Lieutenant-Governor of Scotland with plenipotentiary powers.

Unexpected developments had, however, taken place in Scotland. The English had this time irrevocably offended their Scottish allies; they had forgotten the incontrovertible fact that Charles was not exclusively their king. Argyll's party was willing to bully their king,

A detail of Charles II dancing with his sister Mary at a ball at The Hague, by the Dutch artist Cornelius Janssen. In the background Queen Henrietta Maria and Queen Elizabeth of Bohemia look on (The Royal Collection © Her Majesty The Queen)

insult their king, sell their king. But when the English impertinently killed their king, with hardly so much as by your leave, that was going too far. They proclaimed Charles II in Edinburgh and sent over a party of remarkably grim-looking ministers to ask him to return to Scotland, on terms.

The young king's advisers were bewildered. Montrose, they pointed out, had only his reputation and a handful of officers to place at the king's service. Argyll was master of Scotland. On the other hand, Argyll's terms would hardly make king Charles master of Scotland. He began by asking him to change his religion and went on to insist that the traitor James Graham be expelled from the Court. Montrose had other enemies besides the Covenanters among those about the king. His natural tendency to despise the half-hearted, and the intensity of his desire to serve the king in his own way and no other, did not make him beloved among the fractious, quarrelsome exiles, the failures and the defeated, who made up at least half the following of the young Charles.

The king, in the intrigue-ridden Court in Holland, hesitated for several weeks between the two offers before, in May 1649, he finally appeared to decide for Montrose. Armed with powers to negotiate in the king's name with all foreign princes, and to command all the forces for Scotland by sea and land, Montrose now left The Hague to complete his recruiting operations among the North German and Scandinavian princes.

History has left one tantalizing hint about his short three months in The Hague. Had he fallen in love?

He had spent much of his time, like all distinguished visitors, at the court of the queen of Bohemia. Elizabeth Stuart, sister of Charles I, had been driven with her husband out of Bohemia thirty years before. In spite of debts, poverty, political disasters and her increasing age, this witty, beautiful, headstrong woman had turned her exiled Court at The Hague into the most delightful in Europe. She welcomed Montrose with enthusiasm – a courtier, a soldier, a scholar, and what was more a very good archer, a sport which much delighted her.

The queen had several daughters. Of these, the youngest, Sophie, wrote in later years some entertaining memoirs of her youth. Casting back her mind to that spring of 1649 when she had been seventeen, she wrote that she well remembered Montrose at The Hague. 'Since he was a very brave soldier and a man of high merit, he thought nothing impossible to his management and courage. He was sure he could restore the young king if His Majesty would make him Viceroy of Scotland and, if he did him so great a service, the king could not refuse him the hand of my sister Princess Louise.'

Elizabeth Stuart, Queen of Bohemia

There it is — one astonishing sentence in the memoirs of a lady writing forty years later. But Princess Sophie must have known about her own sister, and why invent such a story?

Princess Louise was a gay, gifted, beautiful creature, high-hearted and adventurous, without vanity or artifice, sincere and impulsive in her actions and too much interested in her favourite pursuit of painting to trouble much about her dress. She had studied under her mother's Court painter, the versatile Gerrard Honthorst, and such of her work as has survived is graceful, vivid and humorous. She was such a woman as Montrose might have loved.

Before he left The Hague Montrose had been painted by Honthorst so that the queen could hang the picture in her cabinet, as she put it, 'to frighten away the Brethren'. This picture, the best-known one of Montrose and the last, certainly shows a face with which a spirited and sensitive woman might have been in love.

Montrose, attributed to Gerard Honthorst (National Galleries of Scotland)

There is just one other relevant fact. After Montrose's death, Louise became a Catholic, secretly left her mother's house and took the veil. Taking the veil is not always the result of a broken heart, but it has been known to be. To do the princess justice, she did not mope her life away, but rose to be an abbess, and guided her convent with energy, conscience and humour for half a century.

The mystery must remain unsolved. Those who prefer to think that Montrose buried all his hopes of love in Magdalen's grave and all his hopes of life in the king's, will always reject this story. Others, however, may hold themselves free to believe that he had this last, unexpected, interlude of dreams and hope before the final tragedy.

On leaving The Hague, Montrose went to North Germany, then to Denmark and Sweden, to get arms, ammunition and ships. In Denmark in July he composed and published an appeal, in the king's name, to the loyal people of Scotland to rise against those who had 'sold their sovereign into death and yet dig in his grave'. The closing passage has a sombre, stormy eloquence:

> Wherefore, all who have any duty left them, to God, their king, Country, Friends, Homes, Wives and Children, or would change, now at the last, the tyranny, violence and oppression of these rebels with the mild and innocent government of the just prince; or revenge the horrid and execrable murder of their sacred king, redeem their nation from infamy, themselves from slavery, restore the present and oblige the ages to come, let them as Christians, subjects, patriots, friends, husbands and fathers, join themselves forth with us. Dead or alive, the world will give them thanks.

The effect of this manifesto on Scotland and the rumours of Montrose's preparations for an invasion caused acute anxiety to Argyll and his party. Soon they issued a counter-proclamation, composed by Warristoun, in which James Graham's past career was described in the foulest terms and a horrible vengeance threatened to the 'miserable miscreant' should he land in Scotland. With more serious consequences, they renewed their overtures to the king. Since Charles had given full powers to Montrose as his Lieutenant-Governor for Scotland, he would have acted more honourably had he refused to receive these overtures. But he was unwilling to neglect any opportunity of regaining his Crown and he mistakenly believed that he could use Montrose's plan of invasion as a threat to compel the Covenanters to give him reasonable terms.

Unhappily, Charles was dealing with men more experienced and more unscrupulous than himself in such affairs. As soon as he agreed to receive them they put it about that he was on the point of abandoning Montrose, a rumour which did great damage to Montrose's preparations at the eleventh hour. The king of Denmark and the Queen of Sweden withdrew much of the promised help and he sailed from Gothenburg early in March 1650 with reduced supplies and a reduced fleet.

Fate was against him. A bad storm scattered his ships and the ammunition vessels were lost before he landed in Orkney. Here in Orkney in March he received the first official intimation from the king of his negotiations with the opposing party.

Charles wrote that he had thought it wise to treat with Argyll's party; this did not mean that he acknowledged them as the true government of Scotland, *although he had had to give them formal recognition for the purposes of the treaty*. None the less, he hoped that Montrose, by winning a speedy victory, would put him in a position to dictate his own terms. He called this 'negotiating with the sword in hand'. As for Montrose himself, wrote the king, 'we require and authorize you to proceed vigorously and effectually in your undertaking, wherein we doubt not but all our loyal subjects of Scotland will cordially join with you.'

Did Charles seriously believe that his loyal subjects of Scotland would flock to join Montrose when they heard that their king had

THE SCOTS HOLDING THEIR YOVNG KINGES NOSE TO Ẏ GRINSTŌ

Come to the Grinstone Charles tie now to late :
To Recolect tis presbiterian fate :.

You Couinant pretenders must Ibee
The subiect of Youer Tradgie Comedie

Jockie

Stoope Charles

This cartoon from a broadsheet of 1651 gives a contemporary view of the relationship between Charles II and the Scots (British Museum)

recognized the government in Edinburgh? It was mere hair-splitting to say that he had only recognized the government for purposes of the treaty. No sooner had Charles made this vital concession than Argyll's party put a price of thirty thousand pounds on Montrose's head *in the king's name*. They issued a statement declaring that Charles had acknowledged their authority and had himself denied that he had ever given any commission to the traitor James Graham.

Thus, in the king's name they called on all the loyal subjects of Scotland to withhold help from the man whom the king himself, according to them, had rejected. What, in the circumstances, were loyal subjects to think?

Montrose understood very well that Charles had cut the ground from under his feet. Yet Charles still wanted him to go on. In a private letter, attached to his more official communication, the king added: 'I conjure you not to take alarm at any reports or messages from others, but to depend on my kindness and to proceed in your business with your usual courage and alacrity.' With this private letter the king also sent the Order of the Garter. It is perhaps the only time that the Garter has been given to soften the effect of a stab in the back.

Montrose answered with a noble restraint:

Sir, I received yours of 12 January with that mark of your favour wherewith you have honoured me, and for which I can make no other acknowledgement but with the more alacrity to abandon my life for your interests, with that integrity that you and all the world shall see that it is not your fortunes, but you, in whatsoever fortune, that I make sacred to serve.

The phrase 'to abandon my life' was no empty flourish. He saw very clearly when he wrote those words that obedience to Charles's orders meant almost certain death.

Yet it would be a mistake to think that the mood of resignation which marks his last letter to the king persisted with him. He had always had a buoyant temperament; he had always believed in his luck; and he had achieved miracles before. His recruiting in Orkney went surprisingly well. He had a staff of experienced officers with him including Colonel Hurry and his old friend Sibbald. A rapid victory of some kind was possible and might yet turn the balance.

In early April he put his men over the Pentland Firth in a fleet of small fishing boats and established a base at Thurso. His plan was to make for Inverness where he believed that the Mackenzies were in arms to join him. His advance was however retarded in the hope of collecting other allies by the way. By 25 April he was in the narrow valley of Carbisdale where it opens towards the Kyle of Sutherland.

The men of Orkney, under the experienced guidance of Montrose's veteran officers, dug themselves trenches and breastworks behind which they could withstand attack, if it came. On the hills to the west the Monroes and Rosses were gathering, with promises to join Montrose.

Here he waited for two days for the clans to complete their mustering and join him. And here, whether because his scouting was bad or because there was treachery, he was surprised on 27 April by one of Leslie's officers, Colonel Strachan, with a small force of picked cavalry.

Strachan's surprise attack need not have been fatal. Tried troops might have stood their ground. The Orcadians, who had never seen cavalry before, flung down their weapons and fled. Montrose had marked a wood a few hundred yards up Carbisdale which he had intended to use as his second line of defence. Sending a message to the Monroes and Rosses to make at once for the wood, he got into it with a small band of his infantry while Strachan was still slashing and cursing his way through the abandoned trenches and the fleeing Orcadians.

Strachan had only three hundred horse. If the Monroes and Rosses had come to Montrose's help he could have redeemed the initial disaster. But they, thinking that Strachan had already won the battle, joined in the attack on Montrose. Like the king, they believed in backing the winner.

Montrose himself, with a few companions, cut his way out of the surrounding forces. They galloped up the glen, then turned the horses loose,

Plan of the Campaign at Carbisdale

meaning to find their way on foot over the moors and hills to the garrison at Thurso.

That morning the weather had been fair. In the afternoon the clouds came down, a thin rain began to fall and it grew very cold. For the next three days and nights mist blotted out the moors. Every stream looked like every other stream; every fold of moor rose up, brown and shrouded, like the one before it. They could not tell where the sun was, whether they were going east or west, north or south. Now and again, they heard the thundering of approaching horsemen and lay low in the heather till the noise died. Strachan had his patrols out for them over all the moors.

Just as legends of Montrose's great campaigns live still in the wild passes of Lochaber and Cairngorm, so do legends of his last flight linger on the high, mournful moorlands which lie between the river Oykell and the lonely waters of Loch Assynt. At one place, they say, he reached a croft and hid under a load of hay while Strachan's men searched. They thrust their muskets into the hay, but missed his body by inches, so that later, when they had gone, he said to the good wife of the place as she gave him a cup of milk: 'I never knew what fear was till now.'

In the four days of his wanderings Montrose had come far to the west. He had separated from his companions, one of whom had died of exposure. He was now in the McLeod country and approaching Loch Assynt, where in the grim little castle of Ardvreck, lived a young chieftain of the McLeods. Only two unadorned historical facts emerge from the mist of doubt and denial which surrounds the capture of Montrose. Ardvreck Castle was the place where he was captured and McLeod of Assynt was the man who handed him over.

Assynt's defenders assert that he found Montrose on the moors, arrested him and sent word to Strachan. It was the straightforward act of a man loyal to the government in power.

A much uglier story was told at the time. It is this: Montrose came

Ardvreck Castle (The Royal Commission on the Ancient and Historical Monuments of Scotland)

to Assynt hungry and exhausted and Assynt took him in with kindness. He even promised him guides to take him back to Thurso when he was well enough to travel. While Montrose lay in the best bed, tired and thankful, Assynt and his wife (perhaps chiefly his wife) bethought them of the blood money for his capture. It was a great deal of money to this poor little chieftain at the back of beyond. So he kept Montrose in false security, with false kindness, and sent word to Strachan.

At the last, with Strachan's men at the door, it is said that Montrose offered Assynt a great sum to let him escape. When that would not do, he asked him at least to kill him cleanly with his sword, that he might not die in Edinburgh 'an object of misery and shame'. This of all things Montrose had feared, that he might fall alive into the hands of his enemies. It was Assynt who made sure that he did.

CHAPTER ELEVEN

THE LAST VICTORY

The lives of some men have a poetic completeness. In ways often unexpected yet strangely right, birth and death, childhood and maturity complete the same design.

Montrose, the late-born, longed-for, only son, had seemed destined always to a fate different from other men. That fate was now unrolling itself to the last syllable. Had the happy, spoilt, ambitious boy had a nightmare vision of how his life would end, would he have believed it, he whose thoughts soared as high as Caesar's and who had chosen for himself the name of Venture Fair? Yet, when every prospect smiled upon him, this happy, spoilt, ambitious boy had written two oddly prophetic lines in his life of Alexander the Great:

So great attempts, heroic ventures shall
Advance my fortune, or renown my fall.

Great attempts and heroic ventures there had been in plenty. The greatest was to come. As soon as the first anguish was over, he saw what he must do and with unswerving resolution set out to do it. He could by the manner of his death set up such a monument to his own integrity and to the king's true service as would make the government of Argyll hateful to all honest men and to all posterity.

Montrose had never swerved from the Calvinist religion which he had sworn to defend when he signed the National Covenant. The central doctrine of Calvinism gave him strength for what lay before him now. He could discern beyond the suffering of the present hour the pre-ordained purpose of a just God.

Skibo Castle as it stands today (The Royal Commission on the Ancient and Historical Monuments of Scotland)

He was too ill to ride. His captors bound him hand and foot and threw him into a cart with a little straw to lie on and a ragged plaid to cover him. For two days they travelled over the rough moorland tracks, and on the second day stopped at Skibo Castle.

And here again we come upon one of the many legends of Montrose. It has the ring of authenticity. The master of the house was away, but his mother, a stern venerable dowager, received them. Life at Skibo Castle was simple, as in most Scots houses; dinner was served for all the household at one long table. The officer in charge of Montrose swaggered in and sat down on the lady's right. Being old and a little puzzled by the visitation, she accepted this at first, but soon her glance, travelling down the table, saw, at the lower end among the servants, two of the soldiers with the prisoner between them. In spite of his old plaid and dishevelled hair, he had very much the air of a gentleman. She asked the officer who he was. Proud of his charge, he told her. Laying down the carving knife which she had just been addressing to a succulent joint of mutton, she requested him to vacate the seat of honour to which he was not entitled and conduct the Marquess to his proper place at her table. The indignant officer answered with some vigour that the traitor, James Graham, could very well stay where he was. Her old eyes blazed. Guests who ate at her table, she said, would sit where she chose; she was not taking orders at her age in her own house. Grasping the joint by the protruding bone, she fetched the impertinent fellow a blow that felled him to the ground. When calm was restored, Montrose was brought to her right hand, the joint was replaced on the dish, and dinner began.

At Tain, Leslie met the prisoner. He had orders from Edinburgh; nothing else explains – and nothing excuses – the treatment he gave Montrose. Feverish from wet and exposure and weakened by neglected wounds, he was mounted on a Highland pony and led in procession through the towns and villages, preceded by a herald proclaiming: 'Here comes James Graham, a traitor to his country.' His enemies thought by this means to make an example of terror to every Royalist in Scotland and to bring Montrose himself and all he stood for into shame and contempt.

The effect was far different, as all who saw him bore witness. These are the words of one of them: 'He sat upon a little shelty horse without a saddle but a quilt of rags and straw, and pieces of rope for stirrups, his feet fastened under the horse's belly, with a halter for a bridle; he wore a ragged old dark reddish plaid. A musketeer [went] on each side. Near Inverness he desired to alight and called for a draft of water, being then in the first crisis of a high fever, and there the crowd from the town came forth to gaze. At the end of the bridge, stepping forward, an old woman exclaimed and brauled [against him]. Yet he never altered his countenance, but, with a majesty and state beseeming him, kept a countenance high.'

Montrose was still young and strong; as his fearful pilgrimage continued in the sunny weather of a beautiful May his fever left him, and his wounds began to heal. On the Sabbath the whole cavalcade halted at Keith. Montrose, bound and guarded, was set before a crowded congregation to hear the minister preach on the fate of Agag, king of the Amalekites, whom the ferocious prophet Samuel commanded to be hewn in pieces. He listened with patience to the torrent of abuse and then, in a momentary pause, interjected the words, 'Rail on, Rabshakeh.' Everyone in that bible-bred audience knew that Rabshakeh was the false priest who tried to seduce the people of Judah from their true allegiance.

It is fair to say that most of the common people and many of the ministers were shocked at the treatment of Montrose. For the few who reviled him in the streets or the pulpit, there were many who treated him with respect and kindness. Leslie, whatever his orders, turned his face the other way when old friends came up to kiss Montrose's hands. At Elgin he even allowed him to have a private talk with a fellow-student of St Andrews days, now a minister, who, in defiance of the excommunication, came to offer him the consolations of religion.

At Pitcapel, where he slept one night, the lady of the house made the guards drunk; then gave him her long cloak and hood and let him out into the night. But his fate was not to be denied. He was stopped by guards in the grounds of the house and brought back. The long road south took them past Kinnaird and here, whether out of kindness or a more subtle cruelty, they stopped to let him see his children. James, his heir, had safely fled abroad, but Robert and Jean, who were ten and eleven, were brought to say goodbye. If they had expected this meeting to break down his constancy, his enemies were disappointed. 'Neither at meeting nor at parting,' wrote our eye-witness, 'could any change of his former countenance [be seen] or the least expression heard, which was not suitable to the greatness of his spirit.'

At Dundee, where the memory of his famous raid was still green, he expected a stony reception, but got the kindest he had yet encountered. They 'furnished him with clothes and all other things suitable to his place, birth and person.' It was in the decent black broadcloth which he received at Dundee that he arrived two days later at the gates of Edinburgh.

While awaiting his arrival, the Committee of Estates had decided on his fate. As it was his resolve to glorify the cause he stood for by his death, so it was theirs to bring it into shame and derision. All the way from Skibo to Dundee the vile project had failed. They were determined to have no such failure in Edinburgh and they laid their plans carefully. Sentence had been passed on him by the Scots Parliament, or rather by the 'ignoble faction' – as Montrose had called it – who controlled Parliament. The sentence fully bore out the threat of a shameful death, which Warristoun had made three months before in his answer to Montrose's manifesto. James Graham was to be hanged at the Market Cross of Edinburgh for three hours on a gibbet thirty feet high; his body was then to be cut down and quartered, the head to be set on the Tolbooth, the limbs on the town gates of Stirling, Glasgow, Perth, and Aberdeen. It was a sentence more insulting even than cruel, for hanging was the fate, not of a nobleman or a soldier, but a criminal.

Montrose was received at the watergate of Edinburgh with news of this grisly sentence, news which, his enemies calculated, would take the majestic calm off his proud face. But he heard it unmoved, saying only that he was sorry they should so dishonour the king's commission.

Meanwhile the people of Edinburgh had been urged by their ministers to take vengeance on the fallen conqueror, the miserable miscreant who had betrayed the Covenant and led Papists and Highlanders against them. The mob, from the beginning, had been very prone to take the law violently into its own hands. By the time Montrose reached the gate, the angry people filled every inch of the narrow Canongate, growling for their prey.

He was aware that he would have the mob to face. But there were still some preliminaries to be got through. Bare-headed, he was made to mount the hangman's cart for the slow procession up the crowded street. No detail had been neglected. A couple of boards had been nailed across the cart on which he was to take his place so that he would be fully exposed for all to see. They made him fast to the boards with several yards of stout rope and ended by tying his arms to his sides so that he would be unable to protect his face from the stones.

These preparations completed, they blew a fanfare, as was usual at fairs when there were camels, lions, or other interesting monsters to show, and the cart creaked forward into the crowd.

For seconds, which seemed like hours, he must have expected the assault of the mob, to whom he was thus offered defenceless. Nothing happened; or rather, everything happened. The angry shouting died away. Silence, in receding waves, travelled up the narrow Canongate.

Montrose paraded through the streets of Edinburgh past the balcony of the Moray House, from where the Marquess of Argyll watched his execution, by James Drummond (National Galleries of Scotland)

With fearful slowness – it took three hours to go less than a mile – the cart lumbered through the crowd. The silence changed its quality. Women began to sob noisily; there were hoarse whispers of admiration, even of blessing. Towards the top of the Canongate there stood (it still stands) a house with a balcony. In this house, on this day of all days, Argyll was celebrating the recent marriage of his son with pomp and feasting. The wedding party crowded on to the balcony to watch the vanquished enemy pass by. At this point the crowd was so thick that the cart came to a standstill. A young woman on the balcony suddenly broke the respectful silence which had fallen with a shrill peal of laughter. Then the mob roared in anger, but not at Montrose. He, meanwhile, was searching the balcony and the windows of the house for a sight of Argyll himself. There indeed he was, not on the balcony, not at any of the large windows, but – very true to character – peeping cautiously through a shutter held ajar.

For a second, perhaps less, the eyes of Montrose met the eyes of Argyll. Then Argyll slammed the shutter to. But the people had seen. A voice shouted above the rest: 'You have not dared to look him in the face these seven years bygone.' All the remaining way to the Tolbooth it was Montrose's triumph. When at last his guards cut the ropes and helped him down, he put two gold pieces into the hangman's hand. 'Thanks,' he said, 'for driving the triumphal car.'

He was handed over to Major Weir, the fanatic commander of the Edinburgh trained bands, a violent, vindictive moody tyrant, who took pleasure in smoking continuously in his prison – for Montrose's dislike of the smell of tobacco was notorious. But scarcely had he reached the small room where he was to spend his last days and taken stock of the pallet bed and barred window, when six ministers appeared at the door announcing that they had come to show him the error of his ways. He made a helpless gesture with his aching arms. 'Gentlemen,' he said, 'the compliments you put on me this day grow something tedious.'

They persisted in arguing with him, that day and the next, which was Sunday, with much insistence on the painful and eternal damnation which awaited him within so short a time. He answered them with surprising courtesy and patience, though not always as seriously as they thought becoming. He was, said one of them later, 'too airy and volage' in his manner.

On Monday he was brought to trial, or rather to hear the sentence formally pronounced. They accused him of high treason in entering Scotland and calling the people of arms, of murder, arson and robbery in his earlier fighting. He answered them not out of any hope of acquittal, but to put on record his truth against their falsehood. He was not speaking to them, but to the absent king, to the people of Scotland, and to history. 'My care hath been always to walk as it became a good Christian and a loyal subject. I engaged in the first Covenant and was faithful to it until I perceived some private persons, under cover of religion, intended to wring the authority from the king.' Speaking of his campaigns for the king, he said: 'Disorders in any army cannot be prevented, but they were no sooner known than punished. Never was any blood spilt but in battle, and even then many thousands live, whom I preserved. I may justly say that never subject acted upon more honourable grounds, nor by a more lawful power, than I did in this service. Therefore, I adjure you to lay aside prejudice, and consider me as a Christian in relation to the justice of the quarrel, as a subject in relation to my royal master's command, and as your neighbour in relation to the many of you whose lives I have preserved in battle. Let me be judged by the laws of God, the laws of nations and nature, and the laws of this land. If you do otherwise, I do here appeal from you to the righteous judge of the world.'

Warristoun, with gloating pleasure, now read out the sentence to which Montrose listened 'with a settled and unmoved countenance'.

Taken back to his narrow prison, he was once again surrounded by the ministers who, in the hope of breaking his spirit at the last, reminded him with detailed comments of the dishonourable death he

Archibald Johnston, Lord Warristoun, by George Jamesone
(National Galleries of Scotland)

would soon endure. 'I am much beholden to Parliament,' he said, 'for the honour they have put upon me. It is a greater thing to have my head upon the Tolbooth for this quarrel, than my picture in the king's bedchamber. Yea, lest my loyalty should be forgotten they have designed lasting monuments to four of the chiefest cities of this realm.'

This silenced his tormentors for a while, though they soon returned to the attack. He would have been glad, as they well knew, not to have to die excommunicate, without the comforts of his religion. But they would neither lift the excommunication nor give him the sacrament until he admitted his guilt in entering Scotland for the king. He remained firm. 'I cannot call that my crime, which I conceive my duty,' he said, and when they began to speak again, he answered them with so passionate a cry of 'Gentlemen, let me die in peace,' that even they were silenced, for a space at least.

The Lady Elizabeth Erskine, wife of Archibald, 2nd Lord Napier (National Galleries of Scotland)

His friends had all been kept away from him, but Lady Napier, young Archie's wife, had managed to send him fine linen and rich clothes so that his last day on earth could be spent with something of that elegance which was so much a part of his character. He was to die on the following morning, 21 May. He had asked his captors to let him have the services of a barber, but this was refused. The thick auburn curls of which he had always been proud were sadly tangled by now, and he was some time arranging them to his satisfaction. The ministers watched this vain proceeding with disapproving eyes. 'Why is James Graham so careful of his head this morning?', one of them mocked him. 'This morning my head is my own,' said Montrose, 'tonight when it is yours you may do with it as you will.'

Soon there was the sound of drums beating. The entire trained bands of Edinburgh were there to escort him to the scaffold. 'Are you afraid of me still?' he asked, and laughed. 'My ghost will defeat you yet.'

The torrential rain which had fallen at daybreak had stopped by the time they were ready for him. He stepped into the street in the grey stormy light of a wet summer day, looking, it was said, like a bridegroom. He was dressed in red, richly laced with silver, a pair of white gloves in his hand, and Brussels lace at his wrists.

The scaffold was erected by the Market Cross, with a gibbet thirty feet high: the three fathom of rope which, in that very place, Rothes had once jestingly predicted. Argyll had no intention of letting him speak to the people. The state of feeling in Edinburgh was quite troublesome enough without that. Montrose himself had not expected any further opportunity. To those near him, and to the one or two friends who had managed to draw close to the scaffold, he said such thoughts as came to him.

To one last onslaught of the ministers he replied: 'I acknowledge nothing! but fear God and honour the king. I have not sinned against man but God, and with Him there is mercy.' He had found that there was no mercy in man. Yet even at the last his natural courtesy prevailed, and speaking with a gentleness almost of apology to his tormentors, he added: 'I desire not to be mistaken as if my carriage at this time in relation to your ways were stubborn. I do but follow the light of my conscience.'

For the king who had deserted him, his only fear was lest he, too, should be betrayed. 'I pray under God he be so dealt withal that he be not betrayed under trust as his father was.' And at last, turning to the people: 'I have no more to say but that I desire your charity and prayers; I shall pray for you all. I leave my soul to God, my service to my prince, my goodwill to my friends, my love and charity to you all.'

They were not empty words. He had never shared the vindictive hatred which inspired most of his adversaries and some of his friends. More than one of the many who saw him go to death recorded with wonder the generosity and grace of his bearing. 'His speech was full of composure and his carriage as sweet as ever I saw a man in all my days,' wrote one spectator.

After he had knelt and prayed at the gallows' foot he rose and looked

Montrose's execution as depicted by E.M. Ward, ARA, for the Commons' corridor, Westminster Palace (from an engraving in the Illustrated London News, *3 February 1855)*

up for one sickening moment at the gaunt gibbet, the long ladder, the rope. With a movement of revulsion he said to the executioner: 'How long must I hang here?'

But his face, when he turned again towards the people, was serene. It was the hangman who was in tears as he tied his hands and hung around his neck the manifesto he had issued in the king's name. As he climbed the ladder, the sun came out between two banks of cloud and struck the scene with momentary glory. From one of the many crowded windows round about, an agent of the English Parliament was watching and writing his report as he watched. He saw the executioner fix the halter; he saw the last brief conversation between the hangman and the victim. At an agreed gesture from Montrose the hangman would push him off the ladder to his death – the horrible process known as 'turning off'.

For a moment more Montrose stood before the people, looking out with calm features and unwavering eyes. The watching Englishman wrote: 'He is just now a turning off from the ladder but his countenance changes not.'

THE GREAT MARQUESS

Montrose was the only one, of all the prisoners taken at Carbisdale and after, who died on the gallows. His friends and soldiers were not spared although they were granted quicker and more honourable death by the axe, or rather by the primitive but merciful guillotine known as the Maiden. Sibbald, Hurry and all his captured officers, all those who had risen for him, were executed, even those few who tried to make their peace with the Kirk. This went on until the people of Edinburgh began to talk of blood sacrifices and refer to the scaffold as the altar of Argyll. Meanwhile, the rank and file of the wretched men of Orkney, herded into Edinburgh, were divided, literally as slaves, among the lords of the 'ignoble faction', who drafted them to work in the mines of Fife.

Thus the savage and ruthless *junto* which had gained control of Scottish affairs piled up a bitter harvest of hatred and brought shame on the nation. An anonymous Scottish poet a few years later summed up what the majority and the best of the nation – whether friends or enemies to Montrose – surely thought of his death.

The poet imagines that he is instructing a messenger who is to carry news from Scotland to the outside world:

> *Ah tell not that he died, nor how, nor why,*
> *Dissuade them in the truth of this to pry,*
> *Befriend us more, and let them ne'er proclaim*
> *Our nobles' weakness, and our country's shame.*

In July 1650 the young King Charles entered Edinburgh as the puppet of Argyll, passing up the Canongate and under the towers of the Tolbooth whence the whitening skull of Montrose looked down. His fateful venture hardly lasted a year. Cromwell defeated Leslie in the field and Argyll's unworthy government gave place to an English military occupation, under General Monck.

The Cromwellian soldiery respected an honourable foe. They left his head on the Tolbooth, but they lifted down his shrivelled limbs from the town gates and laid them decently in church. General Monck took the orphans, Robert and Jean, under his special protection. When their eldest brother came back from France and, at the age of twenty-one, took part in the unsuccesful Royalist insurrection called 'Glencairn's Rising', it was Monck who gave him honourable terms and saw him restored to part of his father's lands.

When Charles II in 1660 was restored to his thrones of England and Scotland, long-deferred vengeance fell on the Marquess of Argyll. But the chivalrous spirit of Montrose lived again in his son, for when Argyll stood his trial before the peers of Scotland, the young Montrose refused to take part less his judgement should be warped by personal feelings.

Argyll was condemned none the less. His questionable services to Charles II could not outweigh the long story of his treachery to Charles I. He was allowed to die decently by the Maiden, and to have his friends and family about him. On the day of his execution he dined formally, with his own servants to wait on him, and he was accompanied to the scaffold with every consolation that his chaplain could give. To do him justice, he showed a quiet resolution, unlike his conduct on the battlefield. He was, in his own way, a deeply religious man, and he had always been convinced of his especial righteousness.

His severed head was placed on the Tolbooth where that of Montrose had been; but even this dishonour was mitigated, for his family had permission to take it down within a week.

It had been well for Scotland had the story of that long conflict between Covenanter and king ended with reconciliation and mercy. It did not do so. The second generation of Covenanters, who suffered under the intolerant government of Charles II and the brutal hand of his minister Lauderdale, paid a heavy price for the errors of their fathers. They have left a record of heroism and endurance which has done much to obliterate the chapter of vengeance and blood written in the name of the Covenant, under Arygll.

What is the place of the Great Marquess in history? Cardinal de Retz perhaps said it as well as anyone when he compared him to a hero of antiquity. He was by temperament and character the type of hero of all the ages, kin to Hector, to Roland, to Lancelot. But these are figures of poetry and romance; Montrose lived in reality, and the very poetry of his nature told against him in a world of prose. Careful and practical he could be and often was, but the springs of his thought and action were poetic and it was perhaps chiefly for that reason that, as a statesman and a man of action, he failed.

His single year of victory earned him a place in local legend, in Gaelic song and Scottish ballad, but it was his death which made him, to all posterity, the Great Marquess; for it was in that last month that the greatness of his nature, responding to the awful challenge, turned the squalid prose of life into a poetic tragedy which few could watch unmoved. It was then that the hero and the poet in him triumphed at once over his weaknesses as a man and the baseness of his enemies.

He earned his place in history and legend not for what he did, but for what he was. The quality of the human soul matters more than the political causes for which men fight and die. Good and evil in politics change from age to age but good and evil in themselves are unchanging. The life and character of Montrose, rightly studied, throw a steady shaft of light on this eternal problem.

In St Giles' Cathedral today lies a statue of Montrose in white marble. The features and the armour have been carefully copied from the portrait by Honthorst. The statue was put there about eighty years ago, when Montrose had long been famous as a Scottish hero, when Sir

The statue of Montrose in St Giles' Church, Edinburgh (Richard Foulsham)

Walter Scott's novel *A Legend of Montrose* had made his character known and loved to generations, and Aytoun's forceful poem 'The Death of Montrose', had fixed some of his noblest sayings in memorable verse. The statue belongs to the age of Queen Victoria, but the sword which is girded to the marble armour, and on which the marble hand lightly rests, may have been his own.

Above the monument a window of richly emblazoned arms commemorates those who fought with him – Gordon and Aboyne, Macdonald, Airlie, Hay of Dalgetty, and all the Graham cousins. In the midst are the red roses and golden sea-shells of the Montrose arms, surmounting the words of the family device: *Ne oublie* – Do not forget.

It was eleven years after his death that Kirk and State in Scotland united to give the Great Marquess burial in St Giles' Cathedral. His friends had gathered his whitened limbs from the four cities of Scotland. They had taken down his head from the Tolbooth and his heart from the silver box in which it had been reverently kept by his eldest son. The precious relic had been rescued by Lady Napier's servants on the night after the execution.

Embalmed with aromatic oils, his body lay in state for a week in the king's own chapel at Holyrood. Then to the sound of trumpets and the muffled beating of drums, fourteen Scots lords bore the coffin up the Canongate. Behind followed the chief officers of state and citizens of Edinburgh, the friends, the soldiers and the servants of Montrose – Black Pate of Inchbrakie, his sons, James and Robert, and all the Graham kin. The trained bands of Edinburgh 'in gallant order ranged both sides of the streets'. Three times they fired a soldier's salute, three times from the castle rock the great cannon thundered and all the bells of Edinburgh gave welcome to Montrose.

A Note on Books and Sources

The greater number of documents for the life of Montrose are to be found in Mark Napier's *Memorials of Montrose*, published by the Maitland Club in 1848–50.

The two principal accounts of his campaigns are those by his chaplain George Wishart and by Patrick Gordon of Ruthven.

There are innumerable contemporary sources both for Montrose's actions and opinions. I have several times in this book emphasized the growth of legend about his name and exploits. But he was not only the subject of legend, he was also the object of propaganda for the last ten years of his life. The historian is thus perpetually faced with contradictory statements, or with several accounts of the same event which cannot be made to tally. The bare truth about Montrose's life has been almost equally obscured by the praise of his friends and the slanders of his enemies.

In a short study of this kind there is no room to set out my reasons for accepting one version of a story or one sequence of events in preference to another. I can only plead (in so far as I may differ from other writers on this subject) that I have selected what seemed to me the most probable.

John Buchan's *Montrose* is, and will long remain, the standard work. Margaret Irwin, in *The Proud Servant* and *The Bride*, has called into being round the figure of Montrose a vivid picture of seventeenth-century society in Scotland and abroad. Sir Walter Scott in his *Legend of Montrose* legitimately subordinates history to the requirements of art; it is not one of his greatest novels but the portrait of Montrose in disguise with which it opens is incomparable.

161

INDEX

Page numbers in italics refer to illustrations
Subentries are given in chronological order

Aberdeen
    anti-Covenant area, 25
    Covenant troops march on, 27
    plundering in, 28
    Battle of Brig o' Dee, 28
    Covenanting army forbidden to sack,
        29–30
    letter from Montrose, *68*
    letter to Montrose, *69*
    Battle of, 70
    Baillie on defensive at, 86
Aboyne, James Gordon, 2nd Viscount
    Battle of Brig o' Dee, 29
    and Montrose, 54, 58, 86, 87, 92
    nd proposed invasion of Scotland, 56
    to wait for news, 60
    Battle of Alford, 95
    raises cavalry, 99, 100
    Argyll's agents influence, 111
    commemorated in cathedral window,
        159
Airlie, James Ogilvie, 1st Earl of, 35, 74,
    101–2, 106, 159
Alford
    Battle of, 95–7, *96*, *97*
    Campaign of, *95*
Anglican Church, 19, 20, 21
Antrim, Randal Macdonnell, 2nd Earl
    and 1st Marquis of
    personality, 24, 54

grant of Kintyre, 24, 54
his plan of action, 54, 56
no news from, 57, 58
and Alasdair Macdonald, 61
Ardvreck Castle, 140, *141*
Argyll, Archibald Campbell, Marquess
    and 8th Earl of, *34*
    dominates Scots Parliament, 33, 42
    political strategist, 33
    Montrose and, 33, 35, 37, 39, 40, 42,
        44, 50, 132, 135, 149
    pedition against Ogilvies, 35, 37
    and deposition of the king, 37, 40
    and Hamilton, 43, 47
    the Incident, 43
    Charles I and, 43, 122
    greatest man in Scotland, 44
    invasion of Galloway, 57
    advances on Dumfries, 57
    and Colkitto Macdonald, 63
    Battle of Aberdeen, 70
    pursues Montrose's army, 70, 72–3,
        74, 101
    letter informing him about Battle of
        Aberdeen, *71*
    Battle of Fyvie, 74
    Montrose's attack at Loch Awe, 76–8
    recalls soldiers from Ireland, 78
    plans to trap Montrose in the Great
        Glen, 80

Battle of Inverlochy, 83–4
Battle of Kilsyth, 101, 102
flees to Berwick, 103
condemns prisoners of war to death, 115
receives 'blood money', 126
and Charles II, 132, 156
executed, 157
Armstrong, Archie, 17
Atholl, 62, 63, 72, 118
Auchinbreck, *see* Campbell of Auchinbreck, Sir Duncan
Auldern, Battle of, 92–4, *93*

Baillie, William
appointed to go against Montrose, 78
Argyll and he plan to trap Montrose, 80
in Aberdeen, 89
in pursuit of Montrose, 90, 100, 101
manoeuvres against Montrose, 94
Battle of Alford, 95, 97
occupies Methven wood, 100
numbers of his forces, 100
Battle of Kilsyth, 102, 103
Berwick
Pacification of, 31
Speed's town plan, *32*
Leven's army rendezvous, 54
Argyll flees to, 104
Leslie reaches, 111
Black Pate, *see* Graham, Patrick
Bond by provost of Jedburgh, *113*
Bothwell Castle, 105, *106*, 108
Brig o' Dee, Battle of, 29
Buchanan Castle, 114

Calvin, John, 20
Calvinism (Presbyterianism) 20, 21, 33, 119, 143
Campbell of Auchinbreck, Sir Duncan, 83, 84
Campbell clan, 24, 76–8, 82, 84, 118
Carbisdale, 138, 139, *139*
Careston Castle, 91
Carlisle, 57, 58, *58*
Charles I, King, *11*
succeeds, 10
neglects Scotland, 10–11
and Hamilton, 11, 13, 47, 54
and Montrose, 13, 35, 38, 51, 56, 106, 108, 122
new Prayer Book, 13, 17
and Scots Kirk, 21, 31
grants land to Lord Antrim, 24
to reduce Scots by force, 25
patches up a peace, 30
Pacification of Berwick, 31
reviews Covenanting troops, 31
and Scots lords, 31
and Scots Parliament, 33, 42–3
Argyll and, 35, 43, 157
Montrose's letters to, *36*, 41, *120–1*
Civil War begins, 45
headquarters at Oxford, 47
Battle of Naseby, 108
and Leslie, 110, 111
surrenders, 119
handed over to English enemies, 126
execution, 129, *129*
Charles II, King, 131
and Montrose, 130, 136, 137–8
proclaimed in Edinburgh, 132
Argyll and, 132, 156

and Argyll's party, 136, 137

cartoon of Charles II and the Scots, *137*

enters Edinburgh, 156

Restoration, 157

intolerant goverment of, 158

Covenanters

increasing strength, 21

Antrim joins, 24

Aberdeen area stirs against, 25

delegation of, 26

growing vindictive intolerance, 32

organized mob violence, 33

Montrose, 33, 50, 86

defenders of Perth, 64

Dundee, 89

quarrel with English Parliamentary allies, 119

and Charles I, 122

'the Engagement', 127

and Charles II, 136

second generation, 158

Covenanting army

marches on Aberdeen, 27

troops' blue ribbon, 27

forbidden to sack Aberdeen, 29–30

Charles I reviews troops, 31

Battle of Tippermuir, 64–5

in occupation of Aberdeen, 70

Battle of Kilsyth, 101, 102–3

Hurry, 118

Cromwell, Oliver, 127, 157

Dee, Old Bridge of, *29*

Deposition by provost of Glasgow, *116–17*

Drummond, William of Hawthornden, 14

Dundee, 89, 90, *90*, 147

Edinburgh

St Giles' Church, *16*, 16–17

new Prayer Book proclamation, 18

Grey Friars Churchyard, 18–19

Huntlys sent as prisoners to, 28

mob violence, 31

Hamilton opens Parliament, 31

Assembly of Scots Kirk, 32

Montrose imprisoned, 42, 149–50

Castle, *42*

Charles I in, 42

Montrose proclaimed traitor, 86

plague, 99

submits to Montrose, 103, 105

Tolbooth prisoners, 103

Charles II proclaimed, 132

Montrose paraded through streets, 147–9, *148*

Charles II enters, 156

Montrose's statue in cathedral, *158*, 159

Montrose's burial, 159–60

Elizabeth I, Queen, 19

Elizabeth Stuart, queen of Bohemia, 132–3, *133*

England

James I and Charles I, 10

absentee Scots in, 11

Anglican Church, 19, 20–1

Puritanism, 20, 21

arms unwillingly, 25

army approaching Border, 38

Fairfax, Sir Thomas, *later* 3rd Baron
    Fairfax, 57
Forth, River, 100
Frasers, 92, 118
Fyvie, Battle of, 74
Fyvie Castle, 73, *73*

Galloway, 54, 57
Glasgow
    High School *or* College, 2, *3*
    Assembly of Scots Kirk, 22
    Montrose enters in triumph, 105
    Proclamation calling Parliament at,
        104
    Montrose calls Parliament, 108
    Leslie holds, 115
    prisoners of war condemned to death,
        115
    deposition by provost, *116–17*
Glen Tilt, near Blair Atholl end, *62*
Glencoe, 79
Gordon, Lord George
    joins Montrose at Elgin, 86–7
    devotion to Montrose, 87, 89
    Battle of Auldearn, 93
    and recall of Gordon cavalry, 94
    Battle of Alford, 95
    death of, 97–8
    commemorated in cathedral window,
        159
Gordon, Nathaniel, 96, 104, 115
Gordon clan
    springs to arms, 28
    Battle of Brig o' Dee, 29
    Battle of Auldearn, 93–4
    Huntly recalls cavalry, 94

Battle of Alford, 95
    returns to Highlands, 111
    gives Montrose no help, 118
Graham, James, *later* 2nd Marquess of
    Montrose, 65, 87, 146, 157,
    160
Graham, Jean, 146, 157
Graham, John, Lord, 65–6, 87
Graham, Sir John, 6, 17–18
Graham, Patrick, *called* Black Pate of
    Inchbrakie
    and Montrose, 61, 63
    raises men, 99, 118
    Montrose's letter of recommendation,
        123
    follows Montrose's coffin, 160
Graham, Robert, 146, 157
Graham family, 5, 17
Great Glen, 80, 81–2, 86
Gretna Green, 56

Hague, The, 130, 132–3
Hamilton, James Hamilton, 3rd
    Marquess and 1st Duke of, *12*
    universally disliked, 11
    character, 11
    and Charles I, 11, 47, 49, 54, 122,
        127
    and Montrose, 12, 47, 49
    power, 13
    and Assembly of Scots Kirk, 21
    opens parliament in Edinburgh, 31
    Argyll and, 43, 47
    under arrest, 54
    Bothwell Palace, 105
    receives 'blood money', 126

'the Engagement', 127
  at Uttoxeter, 129
Hay of Dalgetty, 115, 159
Henderson, Alexander, 22, *23*, 32, 50, 51
Henrietta Maria, Queen, 47, *48*, 126
Highlands, 61, 63, 64, 66, 67
Home, James Home, 3rd Earl of, 111–12
Honthorst, Gerrard van, 133, 158
  portrait of Montrose, *134*
Huntly, George Gordon, 1st Marquess of, *26*
Huntly, George Gordon, 2nd Marquess of, *88*
  in debt to Lorne, 24
  religion, 25
  declares for the king, 26
  and Montrose, 26, 28, 87
  disbands his clan, 27
  calls his clan home, 89, 94
  gives Montrose no help, 118
Huntly Castle, *27*
Hurry, Sir John
  in pursuit of Montrose, 91
  Highland reinforcements, 92
  Battle of Auldearn, 93–4
  and Montrose, 118, 138
  executed, 156

Inverary, 76, 77
Inverness, 118
Inverlochy
  Campaign of, *78*
  Argyll and Auchinbreck at, 81
  Inverlochy Castle, *83*

Battle of, 84
Ireland, 43, 45, 78

James VI, King of Scots, *afterwards* James I of England, 10, 21
Jedburgh
  bond by provost of, *113*
Johnstone, Archibald, 33

Kilchurn Castle, 77
Kilsyth
  Campaign of, *99*
  Battle of, 101–3, *102*
Kincardine Castle, *119*
  Grahams' principal castle, 6
  Montrose family at, 14, 45
  Brechin Cathedral, 17
  Rollo at, 50
  razed, 118
Kinnaird Castle, 7, *7*, 72, 123, 146
Kintyre
  Charles I grants to Antrim, 24
  Antrim and, 54
  Irish Macdonalds land in, 61
  Colkitto Macdonald driven from, 63
  Alasdair Macdonald, 114, 115
Knox, John, 21

Laud, William, Archbishop of Canterbury, 13, 24
Lauderdale, John Maitland, 1st Duke of, 158
Leslie, Alexander, 1st Earl of Leven, *25*
  commands Scots forces, 25, 38, 45

permits plundering, 28

well-ordered army, 30

and Charles I, 31

created Earl of Leven, 43

York hard pressed by, 57

Scots government sends message for help, 86

Leslie, David, *later* 1st Baron Newark, *110*

Montrose and, 110, 111, 145, 146

Battle of Philiphaugh, 112

clemency, 114

will not be manoeuvred into battle, 114

Cromwell defeats, 157

Linton, John Stewart, Lord, *later* 2nd Earl of Traquair, 111, 112

Lithgow, William, 2

Lochaber, 81, 82

Loch Awe, 76, 77

Loch Leven, 80, 81

Lorne, Archibald Campbell, Viscount, *later* Argyll, 8th Earl of, *q.v.*, 22, 24

Loudon, John Campbell, 1st Earl of, 104

Louise of Bohemia, Princess, 133, 135

M'Corquodales, 76–7

Macdonald, Alasdair, *later* Sir Alasdair

leader of Irish forces, 61

in Atholl, 62

appearance, 63

his aim, 76

Battle of Auldearn, 92–3

receives accolade, 108

sent to recruit, 110

withdraws his help, 114–15

commemorated in Cathedral window, 159

Macdonald, Colkitto, 63

Macdonalds, Irish

Antrim's plan of action, 54, 56

fighters, 56

no sign of, 57

land in Kintyre, 61

Atholl clans and, 62

Montrose and, 63

numbers, 64

Roman Catholics, 67

at Aberdeen, 70

and Scots clansmen, 76

Macdonalds, Scots

Campbells and, 24

and Montrose, 76

Macdonalds of Keppoch, 81

killed at Inverlochy, 81

Battle of Inverlochy, 84

Battle of Auldearn, 93, 94

Battle of Alford, 95

Battle of Kilsyth, 101

Battle of Philiphaugh, 114

officers brought to trial, 115

Mackenzies, 92, 118, 138

Macleod of Assynt, 140, 142

Mar, John Erskine, 3rd or 8th Earl of, 100

Marston Moor, Battle of, 58

Maurice, Prince, 126

Middleton, John, 118

reinforcements, 29

and Roxburgh and Home, 111–12

clemency, 114, 115

Montrose makes terms with, 122

Monck, George, *later* 1st Duke of Albemarle, 157

Montrose, *seaport*, 14, 73, 87, 125

Montrose, James Graham, 5th Earl and 1st Marquess of, *frontispiece, xii, 134*

character: ambition, 4; candour, 56; caution and stubbornness, 64; charm, 67, 127; chivalry, 32; courtesy, 67, 153; daring, 82; determination, 60; dignity, 127; frankness, 33; as a general, 99; generosity, 1–3, 7; honour, 30, 115; magnanimity, 105–6; military gifts, 30, 67; organizer and leader, 56; skill, 82; sweetness of nature, 5; vanity, 4–5

at St Andrews University, 1–2, 4

writes verse, 4, 47, 49, 52–4, 130

appearance, 4, 63, 152, 153

Scotland's elder statesmen and, 6

recreations, 6–7

his sword, 5, 159

and his wife, 7, 52–4, 125

sojourn on the Continent, 9–10

Hamilton and, 11, 13, 47, 49–50

Charles I and, 13, 31, 50, 51, 57, 106, 108, 122

home life, 14, 45

opposition to new Prayer Book, 18

given high command, 25

and Covenanters, 26, 33

Huntly and, 26, 28, 94

Leslie's second in command, 27

marches on Aberdeen, 27

troops' blue ribbon, 27

Battle of Brig o' Dee, 29

and Argyll, 35, 37, 39, 40, 50, 70, 72–4, 132

popularity, 35, 43

reputation damaged, 35

letters to Charles I, *36, 41, 85, 120–1*

moderate party takes shape, 37

Cumbernauld Bond, 37–8, 40

loyalty to Covenant, 38, 56

crosses Tweed, 38

Stewarts' witness against, 41

released, 44

political ideas, 45

warns Henrietta Maria, 47

Henderson and, 50, 51

religious convictions, 50

Antrim's plan of action, 54, 56

recruiting, 56, 57, 108

manifesto, 56–7

and Prince Rupert, 58

north to the Highlands, 60

at Tulliebelton, 61

and Atholl clans and Irish Macdonalds, 63

raises Royal Standard, 63

composition of his army, 64, 74

Battle of Tippermuir, 65

and his children, 65–6, 87, 146

military problems, 66–7

tactics, 67, 89

letter to Aberdeen Town Council, *68*

Battle of Aberdeen, 70

Battle of Fyvie, 74

back to Blair Atholl, 75

invasion of Campbell country, 76–8

reiterates orders against bloodshed, 78

crossing of Loch Leven, 80, 81

march to Inverary, 78, 80–3

insists on retaining trumpet, 83

Battle of Inverlochy, 84

his prisoners, 84, 103, 105, 115

and Lord George Gordon, 87, 98

takes Dundee, 89

retreat from Dundee, 90–2

Battle of Auldearn, 92–4

counter-manoeuvres against Baillie, 94

Battle of Alford, 95

crosses Forth, 100

letter to Lord Ogilvie, 107

Battle of Kilsyth, 101–3

his conduct as conqueror, 105–6

reviews his army, 108–9

and (David) Leslie, 110–11, 114, 145

Battle of Philiphaugh, 112, 114

his followers condemned to death, 115

makes terms with Middleton, 122

beloved by his troops, 122

leaves Scotland in exile, 125

suggests new invasion of Scotland, 126, 130

and execution of Charles I, 129–30

Charles II and, 130, 132, 136, 137–8

Elizabeth of Bohemia and, 132–3

and Princess Louise, 133, 135

appeals to Scots to rise, 135

lands in Orkney, 136

price put on his head, 137

Carbisdale skirmish, 139

at Ardvreck, 140, 142

journey under capture to Edinburgh, 143–7

paraded through Edinburgh streets, 147–9, 148

in prison, 149–50

final days, 150, 152–4

execution, 154, 155

monument, 158, 159

burial, 159–60

insignia, 160

Montrose, Magdalen, Countess of, 124

marries, 7

children, 14, 123

and Montrose, 52–4

legend about, 123, 125

Napier, Sir Archibald Napier, 1st Baron, 37

Montrose and, 4, 37, 41, 106

arrested, 41

released, 44

Napier, Archibald, later 2nd Baron Napier, 95, 96, 103, 118

Napier, Lady, 152, 152, 160

Napier, Margaret Graham, Lady, 38

National Covenant

contents, 19

copies broadcast, 19

Henderson, 22

Huntly signs, 28

signing made compulsory, 32

Montrose, 35, 38, 56, 143

Ogilvies, 35

Charles I and, 43

Newark Castle, 114

Newcastle, 39, 58, 126

Speed's town plan, 39

Nottingham

Royal Standard raised, 45, 46

O'Cahan, Seumas, 111, 115

Ogilvie, James, Lord, *afterwards* 2nd Earl of Airlie, 51, 58, 60, 106, 115
Ogilvie, Lady, 37
Ogilvie clan, 35, 102
Orkney, 136, 138, 139
    fate of Orcanians, 156
Oxford, 47, 51–2, 54, 86
    Christ Church, *51*

Parliament, English, 45, 47, 54, 86, 119
Parliament, Scots
    Hamilton opens, 31
    Committee of Estates, 33, 40, 41
    under Argyll's domination, 33
    Montrose opposes Argyll, 35
    and Charles I, 42–3
    Montrose's coat of arms defaced, 86
    Proclamation calling Parliament at Glasgow, *104*
    Montrose calls, 108
    Lady Montrose petitions, 123
    sentences Montrose, 147
Pepys, Samuel, 130
Perth, 64, 65
Philiphaugh, Battle of, 112–13, *112*
Prayer Book, *15*
    new, 13
    Scots attitude to, 14, 16–17
    proclamation on, 18
    Assembly of Scots Kirk protests against, 22
    Charles I and, 43
Presbyterianism, *see* Calvinism

Retz, Jean de Gondi, Cardinal de, 127
Richelieu, Arman Jean, Cardinal duc de, 9
Richmond, 58
Robertson clan, 62, 64, 67
Rollo, Sir James, 2nd Lord Rollo, 50
Rollo, Sir William, 60, 86, 115
Rothes, John Leslie, 6th Earl of, *18*
    and new Prayer Book, 17, 18
    and Charles I, 31
    jovial good humour, 32
    death, 33Roxburgh, Robert Ker, 1st Earl of, 111–12
Rupert, Prince, Count Palatine of the Rhine, 52, 57–8, 59, 126

St Andrews
    Gordon's map of, *2*
Scotland
    neglected by James VI and Charles I, 10–11
    new Prayer Book, 13, 14, 16–17
    Grahams and freedom of, 17
    Calvinism, 19, 21
    Kintyre granted to Lord Antrim, 24
    Scots take up arms, 25
    Scots lords suspect a trap, 31
    Scots army, 45
    and English Parliament, 47, 54
    army crosses Border into England, 56
Scots Kirk
    Assembly of, 21, 22, 32
    Montrose and, 33, 50
    Montrose excommunicated, 86
Seaforth, George Mackenzie, 2nd Earl of, 80, 81

Sibbald, William, 60, 138, 156

Silver medal, archery prize, *1*

Skibo Castle, *144*, 144–5

Solemn League and Covenant, 54, *55*

Sophie of Bohemia, Princess, 133

Stewart, John, of Dunkeld, 40–1

Stewart, Walter, 41

Stewart clan, 62, 64, 67

Strachan, Colonel, 139, 140

Sword, Montrose's, *5*, 159

Sydserf, Thomas, Bishop of Orkney, 11, 13

Sydserf, Tom (Montrose's steward), 8, 9, 11, 86

Traquair, Sir John Stewart, 1st Earl of, 111

Traquair, young, *see* Linton, John Stewart, Lord

Tweed, River, 38

Wallace, Sir William, 6

Warristoun, Archibald Johnston, Lord, 135–6, 147, 150, *151*

Weir, Major, 149

Whitford, Walter, Bishop of Brechin, 17

Wishart, George, 108, 127, 129, 130
title page of *Montrose*, *128*

Tippermuir, Battle of, 65

Tippermuir and Perth, Campaign of, *65*

York, 47, *49*, 56, 57
Speed's town plan, *49*

THE DEUCALIDON SEA

THE KINGDOME OF SCOTLAND

James King of Great Britain, Fraunce & Ireland.

Henry Prince of Wales & Ireland.

Rona Iland

LEWYS

The Yles of Hebrides Caled of Pliny Hæbudes, of Beda Meuaniae

SKYE

Assin Shire

Loquhaber

Argile

THE IRISH SEA

PART OF IRELAND